# FARINA MG AND RILEY SALOONS

## NEIL CAIRNS

AMBERLEY

First published 2024

Amberley Publishing
The Hill, Stroud,
Gloucestershire, GL5 4EP

www.amberley-books.com

Copyright © Neil Cairns, 2024

The right of Neil Cairns to be identified as the Author
of this work has been asserted in accordance with the
Copyright, Designs and Patents Act 1988.

All rights reserved. No part of this book may be reprinted
or reproduced or utilised in any form or by any electronic,
mechanical or other means, now known or hereafter invented,
including photocopying and recording, or in any information
storage or retrieval system, without the permission in writing
from the Publishers.

ISBN: 978 1 3981 1574 3 (print)
ISBN: 978 1 3981 1575 0 (ebook)

British Library Cataloguing in Publication Data.
A catalogue record for this book is available from the British Library.

Typeset in 10pt on 13pt Celeste.
Typesetting by SJmagic DESIGN SERVICES, India.
Printed in the UK.

Appointed GPSR EU Representative: Easy Access System Europe Oü, 16879218
Address: Mustamäe tee 50, 10621, Tallinn, Estonia
Contact Details: gpsr.requests@easproject.com, +358 40 500 3575

# Contents

Foreword   4

Acknowledgements   7

Introduction   8

1 History   12

2 Selling the Cars   29

3 The Different Models   34

4 Riley 4/68 and MG Magnette Mk3   41

5 MG Magnette Mk4 and Riley 4/72   48

6 Modifications During Production   58

7 The BMC B Series Engine   62

8 Problems with Farinas   76

9 The Riley Silhouette and Riviera   80

10 The Di Tella MG   83

11 The Past and the Future   89

# Foreword

In all the long history of the MG, a car name famous all over the world, no other models were as tenacious as the Farina Magnettes. It is a car that if you brought it up in conversation with MG enthusiasts, you were liable to find yourself left alone in the corner of the room. Such was the dislike of this car in the MG world that today very few recent aficionados have even heard of it. The bad name it gained upon the introduction of the MG Magnette Mk3 in late 1958 was a little harsh on the model; after all, it did go on to sell 31,004 between 1959 and 1968. The total production of the numerous Farina BMC models was over 900,000 between 1959 and 1971. The much better car it replaced, the Z series Magnette, sold 36,601 between 1953 and 1959.

In adverts, it was claimed to be the first MG available with a Borg Warner type 35 automatic gearbox (later shared with the MGB). Wilson McComb pointed out in *Safety*

The MG Magnette Z series sold more cars in fewer years than the Farina model.

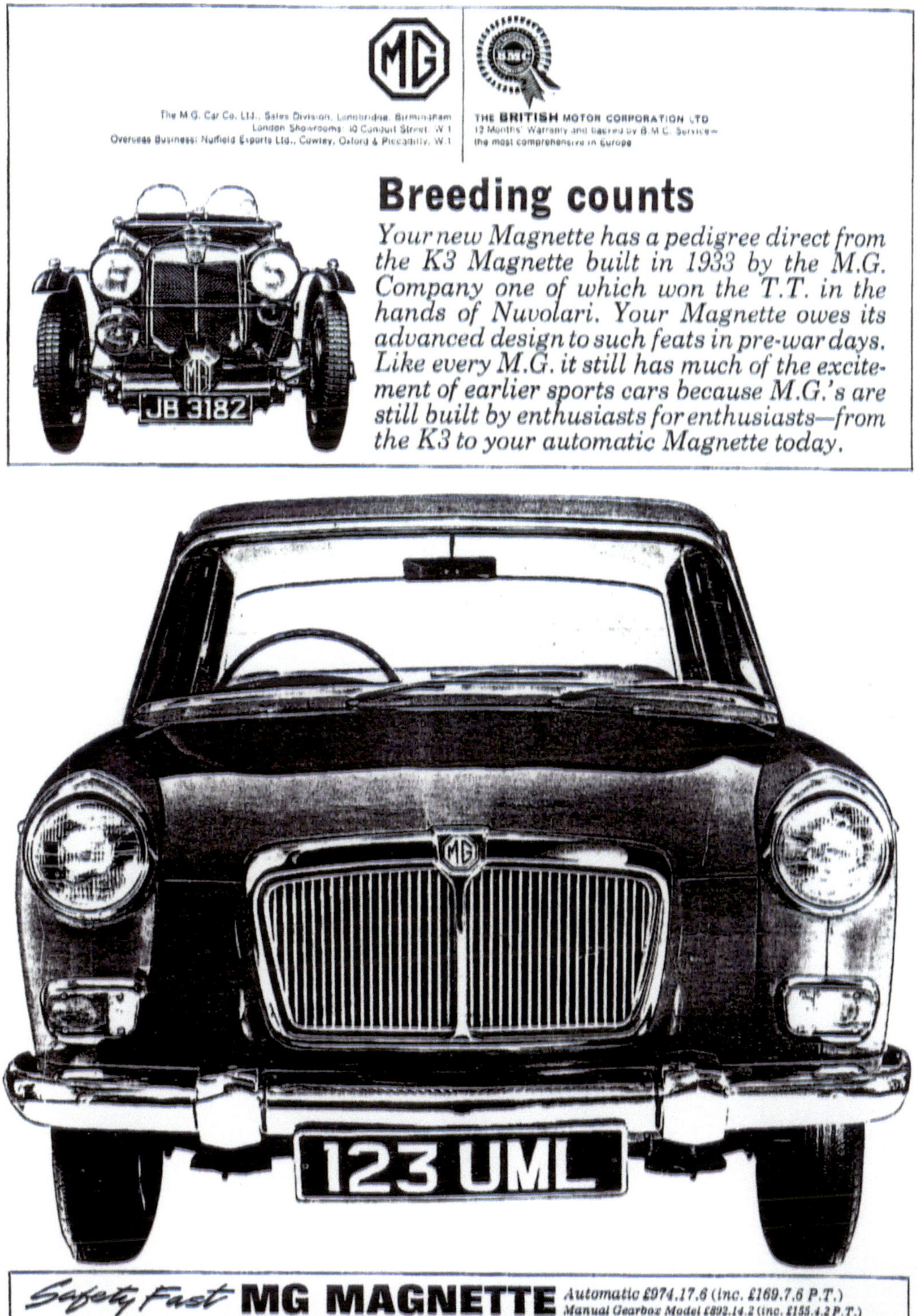

## Breeding counts

*Your new Magnette has a pedigree direct from the K3 Magnette built in 1933 by the M.G. Company one of which won the T.T. in the hands of Nuvolari. Your Magnette owes its advanced design to such feats in pre-war days. Like every M.G. it still has much of the excitement of earlier sports cars because M.G.'s are still built by enthusiasts for enthusiasts—from the K3 to your automatic Magnette today.*

*Safety Fast* **MG MAGNETTE** — Automatic £974.17.6 (inc. £169.7.6 P.T.) / Manual Gearbox Model £892.14.2 (inc. £155.4.2 P.T.)

The advert in 1958 that caused MG enthusiasts to complain. Today it would not get past the ASA.

*Fast*, the MG Car Club's magazine: 'It is interesting to remember that the very first MG Magnette, the K series saloon of 1932 was at first not sold with a manual gearbox, but with semi-automatic Wilson pre-selector unit as standard.' The slogan 'breeding counts' appeared in an advert in many car magazines of the time, claiming the Farina owed much of its advanced design to that earlier racing K3. The only things the two cars shared, however, were the MG badge and the automatic gearbox idea.

Though, of course, MG did begin as a garage who modified Morris Oxfords back in the early 1920s. So, being a modified Morris Oxford, the Farina Magnette was only following in the footsteps of that first model.

The Farina MG is only a modified Morris Oxford, just like the very first MGs were.

# Acknowledgements

There is no way any book like this can be written without recourse to the experiences and photos of other like-minded people. Where I have used a photo not my own, the name of its contributor is credited in the caption. Images have been used from Alejandro Mogni of Cordoba, Argentina for the Di Tella, the MG Car Club records and the British Motor Industry Heritage Trust.

©BMIHT. All publicity material and photographs originally produced for/by the British Leyland Motor Corporation, British Leyland Ltd and Rover Group, including all its subsidiary companies, is the copyright of the British Motor Industry Heritage Trust and is reproduced here with their permission. Permission to use images does not imply the assignment of copyright, and anyone wishing to reuse this material should contact BMIHT for permission to do so.

Every attempt has been made to seek permission for copyright material used in this book. However, if we have inadvertently used copyright material without permission/acknowledgement we apologise and will make the necessary correction at the first opportunity.

# Introduction

When the five BMC models of the Austin Design Office model No. 9 (ADO9G for the MG, ADO9R for the Riley) were released to the press in late 1958 and early 1959, there were many complaints of 'badge engineering'. The *Times* and *Telegraph* newspapers, as well as the *Motor* and *Autocar* motoring magazines, were full of letters from readers. The main thread of them all was that all the models looked the same and had the same mechanicals, but with different marque badges on the radiator grille. BMC were building a car that would suit many customers who were loyal to their particular brand. Today we have the various 'World Cars' of the big car companies. Again, these are the same car but with different badges, such as Opel and Vauxhall, and with what were known as the Astra, Nova, and Cavalier with another name and badge in other countries. BMC did not realise it at the time, nor did the UK public, but the ADO9 series was one of the first 'World Cars'. They cannot claim a first, as Rolls-Royce beat them to it with their dual Rolls-Royce and Bentley models, with only the radiator, rocker cover, and badge differing in their 1952 all-steel saloon. Daimler and Lanchester shared models in the 1950s, as did Jaguar and Daimler later. Morris and Wolseley models have been virtually identical since the early 1930s, so why all the fuss in 1958?

Austin were not excluded either, with their little Austin Seven sold in the UK retailed as a BMW Dixi in Germany (BMW's first car) and the Rosengart in France. MG took over an Austin model in 1958, the little Austin Healey Sprite, and stuck an MG badge on it, calling it a Midget. Badge engineering, as it was called, was practised by many companies. The Rootes Group were at it in the 1930s, with big Humbers wearing the Talbot badge and Hillmans wearing Singer badges. After the Second World War they too used one bodyshell for their Hillmans, Singers, Sunbeams and Humbers. By the 1970s they ran these with virtually identical models, having just the badge and some trim differing.

BMC caught all the flack back in 1959 with their Austin A55 Mk2, Morris Oxford series 5, Wolseley 15/60, Riley 4/68 and the MG Magnette Mk3. However, it must have been successful, as the 1100-1300 that followed included a Vanden Plas version as well as these other five BMC names, and they sold in the millions. BMC had in fact tried out the market for similar models with a differing specification with the Palmer-designed MG Z series Magnette in 1953. This had been beaten onto the market by the Wolseley 4/44 in 1952. The Wolseley used a 46bhp Nuffield 1,250cc XPAW engine (with a different sump) from

Badge engineering was common practice in the 1950s and 1960s.

BMW's first car was a licence-built Austin Seven called the 'Dixi'.

the 1952 MG YB saloon, with the YB gearbox, rear axle and brakes. The gearbox had been modified to column change. The Z Magnette used a redesigned 1,200cc Austin Cambridge A40 engine, gearbox and rear axle. It was the first use of the BMC B series engine, in larger 1,489cc form, twin SU carburettors and 60bhp. Both the Wolseley 4/44 and MG Z Magnette sold well. So, in 1958, BMC announced the replacement model for all its mid-range saloon cars, based on the floor pan and running gear of the 1957 Austin Cambridge A55.

Over the years many motoring history writers have spoken poorly of this MG, though few have driven one and even fewer have owned one. Once you give a dog a bad name, others will follow your lead.

Many know of the Morris Oxford being exported to India to become the Hundustan – it is still a common taxi there these days but now has a Japanese engine and no longer a BMC B series. Few, however, know of the export of the MG Farina Magnette and Riley 4/68 to Argentina, where the car was first a CKD assembly (arrived in boxes and assembled there), eventually using quite a lot of locally sourced items. Even fewer know of the specialist Farina Riley, which was built in Salisbury by Wessex Motors.

Surely the Mk3 and Mk4 MG Magnettes could not be that bad? After all, it did have the MGA's engine, gearbox and rear axle, along with the Austin Healey 1000 front suspension and steering (also used on the Austin FX4 taxi). If only the MG Z Magnettes had not been such a good car.

The original MG Magnettes were expensive six-cylinder racing cars built in single numbers in the 1930s. The name was used again on the 1953 MG Magnette ZA saloon and MG enthusiasts complained. Interestingly, MG always used the letters of the alphabet to denote each model, but the Austin-based Mk3 and Mk3 Magnettes did not have such a denomination. It was a bit of a poor man's Rover, but the Farina Riley was aimed at that market.

Few books on MGs even mention the Farina MG Magnette or the 4/68 and 4/72 Rileys; those that do only tend to have a small paragraph on the cars. So, here is a better story.

MG had entered the big saloon car market in the 1930s.

*Above*: A line up of 1950s MG saloons. The Farina MG followed the Y Type and Z series.

*Below*: The Farina Riley did not suffer the same criticism that the MG had. It did fulfil the Gentleman's Fast Saloon image well.

# 1
# History

In 1947 Austin built their first all-new model after the Second World War. It was the A40 Devon model – the '40' was the brake horsepower (bhp) of the engine. The Devon was the four-door model, while the Dorset was the two-door. It had a separate chassis with independent front suspension by unequal wishbones with an Armstrong lever-arm damper as the upper arm. It used pre-war worm-and-peg steering with an idle box and track control arms, resulting in a multitude of ball joints. This was not a recipe for accurate steering, though a similar system was fitted to the Austin Healey sports cars later. The A40 was, like a great percentage of British cars then, exported to the USA in large numbers. The United

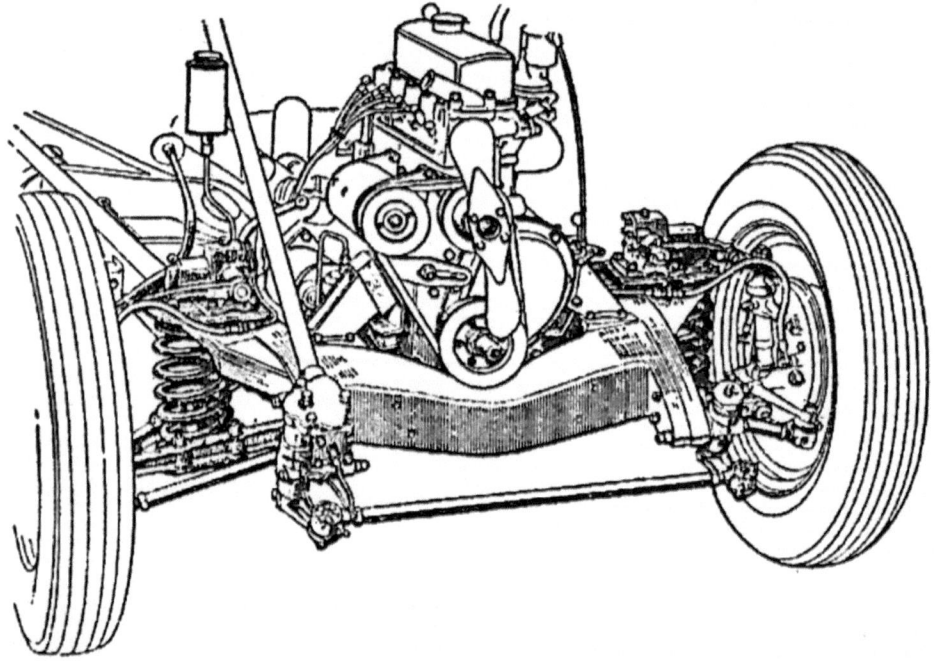

The Austin A40's multitude of ball joints gave fairly vague steering.

Kingdom was then in desperate need of dollars. The engine was of 1,200cc overhead valve (OHV) and developed from the Austin 16. Many of these USA vehicles ended up as second cars for the lady of the house. Using such a tiny engine on the vast roads of the USA was tantamount to cruelty. Between 1947 and 1951, 100,000 were sold.

By 1952 the A40 was restyled as the Somerset and looked like a smaller A70. The Somerset was wider inside but used basically the same running gear, though with an extra 2bhp (should it have been the A42?). The redesigned engine became the 1,200cc version of the now famous BMC B series, first seeing use as the 1953 MG Magnette ZA in 1953 as a 1,489cc unit.

In 1956 Austin designed its new A50 as a monocoque chassisless car. The structure used the same measurements as the A40. This was so the suspension and running gear of the A40 Hampshire could be reused with little difficulty and the production line need not have too much alteration. Austin was very late in coming to what is called monocoque construction, where the whole car body is the main structure with no separate chassis. This Austin product was not a particularly efficient structure, unlike the very clever little Austin A30/A35 that used an almost aircraft-type stressed shell. At first the new structure was so weak it broke up at attachment points of the suspension, so a replica of the old A40 chassis as floor-runners was welded to the floor pan to stiffen it. It was this A50 floor pan that was later used on the A55 and the 1959 on Farina A55 Mk2 cars. The A55 used the 1,489cc BMC B series engine with 55bhp; the A50 used a 50bhp version.

Whilst the A40 was being updated to its more rounded Somerset version, in 1952–53 the Austin and Morris companies were arranging to be merged, with Austin coming out as the dominant company and Morris a poor second. The new company was called the British

Austin A40 Devon.

*Above*: Austin A40 Somerset.

*Below*: Austin A50, a chassisless car that originally required extra stiffening of its underframe.

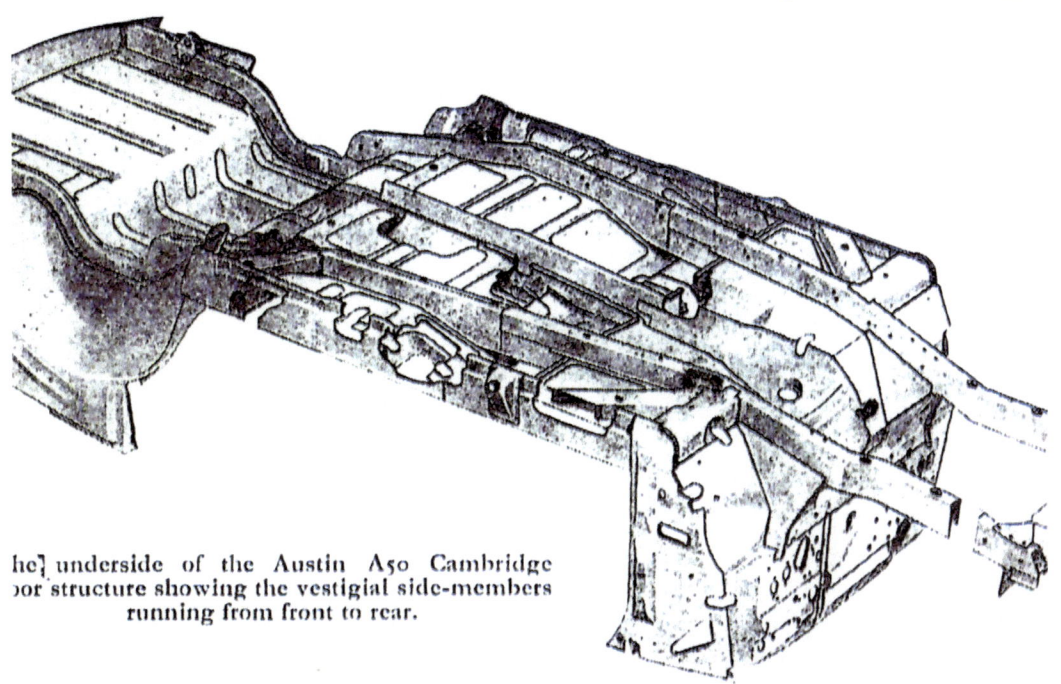

he] underside of the Austin A50 Cambridge
)or structure showing the vestigial side-members
running from front to rear.

The underframe of the A50 with the same layout as the chassis of the A40.

Motor Corporation, or BMC for short. This meant that as time passed much of the original Morris (hence Nuffield) engineering was cast aside and Austin items were fitted instead. This is seen in the 1953 MG Magnette ZA being fitted with a BMC B series 1,489cc engine and Austin gearbox with a BMC banjo rear axle. It may have been a Nuffield design by Gerald Palmer, but underneath it was all basically Austin. Standardisation was a very good thing for ease of production and the need of fewer spares holdings for franchised garages.

During the amalgamation of the Morris and Austin empires (Morris included Wolseley, MG and Riley) at the Nuffield organisation, as Morris had become in the 1930s, there were new models about to be introduced. These had been designed by Gerald Palmer as a family and consisted of the MG Magnette, Wolseley 4/44, Riley Pathfinder and Wolseley 6/90. The Wolseley 4/44 used the SC/2 XPAG engine (with a modified sump) from the pre-war designed MG Y type, model YB of 1,250cc. The Wolseley 6/90 got the new six-cylinder BMC C series of 2,300cc. The Riley kept its 2,443cc four-cylinder pre-war high-camshaft OHV engine, and the MG Magnette used the BMC B series four cylinder. So, two Nuffield cars had old Nuffield engines and two had new BMC engines. By 1956 the old Nuffield engines had gone, the Riley Pathfinder was now a Wolseley 6/90 with a different grille and the 4/44 gained a single carburettor 1,489cc BMC engine to become the 15/50. The mechanical 'Austinisation' of Morris cars was now complete. All that remained was to standardise the bodies.

Why you ask? Well, with the amalgamation of Austin, Morris, Wolseley, Riley and MG, very few garages held franchises for all five makes, so proved to be a good business plan to be able to supply all of them with their make of car. This would enable having a standard set of spares that would be easily backed up, requiring small spares holdings by the garages. The original design was none too sharp, and on a visit to the factory the Duke of Edinburgh made a comment to that effect. This made Len Lord reappraise his stylists and bought in Pinin Farina of Italy whose much more up-to-date style was adopted – hence the nickname 'the Farina models'.

BMC invited a number of the franchise garage managers to Longbridge to see their newest model on 12 November 1958. The MG was the first of the Farina-styled cars to be shown to them. The press were shown the car early in 1959 and the first appearance to the public was in the *Autocar* and *Motor* magazines in March 1959. The Mk3 MG Magnette was seen by those who were to sell. The Riley 4/68 followed it on 3 February 1959. Both cars shared their bodies, running gear, and most of their trim. The 4/68 was better fitted out for its driver, with a cable-driven tachometer and wood veneer dash. The

On 12 November 1958 the first of the new Farina models, the MK Mk3 Magnette, was shown to the garage proprietors who sold BMC cars.

MG shared its instrument with the preceding ZB MG saloon. BMC had a 'New Model Introduction' show for each Farina model, which must have become a bit of a bore for the garage proprietors, who were supposed to be excited at each separate unveiling, if you had franchises for all five.

Austin had merged with Morris in 1952–53 to improve their chances on the world markets, being up against huge USA giants like Ford and General Motors (GM). Rumour had it BMC, the newly formed company, was now the fifth-largest motoring manufacturer in the world. Old UK names like Wolseley, Riley, MG, Morris, Austin, and Vanden Plas were now under one management. Or, at least, that was the idea. In fact, BMC were just a holding company and struggled to get all the small individual firms to pull together. Riley remained virtually independent right up until the 1959 Farina 4/68. Leonard Lord

The press were invited to see the cars in early 1959 and were not too impressed with the obvious similarities of them all.

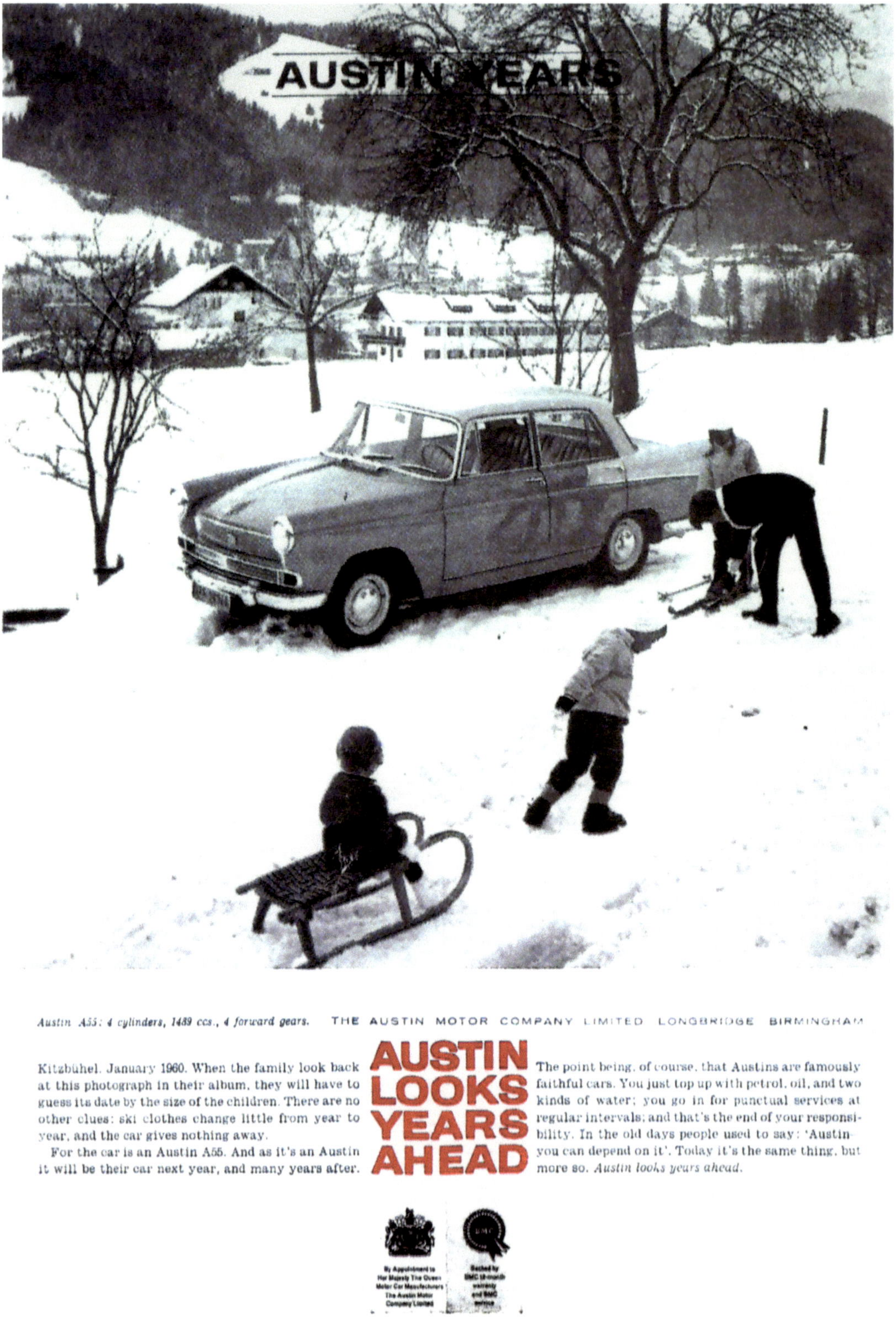

## THE AUSTIN YEARS

Austin A55: 4 cylinders, 1489 ccs., 4 forward gears.     THE AUSTIN MOTOR COMPANY LIMITED   LONGBRIDGE   BIRMINGHAM

Kitzbühel. January 1960. When the family look back at this photograph in their album, they will have to guess its date by the size of the children. There are no other clues: ski clothes change little from year to year, and the car gives nothing away.

For the car is an Austin A55. And as it's an Austin it will be their car next year, and many years after.

### AUSTIN LOOKS YEARS AHEAD

The point being, of course, that Austins are famously faithful cars. You just top up with petrol, oil, and two kinds of water; you go in for punctual services at regular intervals; and that's the end of your responsibility. In the old days people used to say: 'Austin you can depend on it'. Today it's the same thing, but more so. *Austin looks years ahead.*

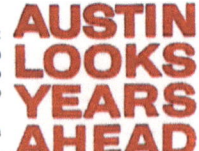

The Austin A55 Mk2 version of the new Farina saloons.

was the leading light of the firm, its managing director, and he worked hard to improve the management. The arrival of the ADO9 was proof of his success and regarded as very forward looking. There were valid criticisms of the MG and Riley versions, as road holding was not of the best on the staid Austin A55, even though the Austin Healey 100-3000 used the same suspension components. Whilst the sports car Healey had a very low centre of gravity, the Farinas were very over-bodied and a bit top heavy. It was not until 1962 that BMC eventually improved the models because of the media's bad reviews. BMC added anti-roll bars, front and rear, double acting dampers, lowered the car an inch all round and added a longer and wider wheelbase. Sadly, one or two ex-MG ZB owners who purchased the early versions of the Mk3 Magnette returned them and asked for their old car back. It was true to say the Mk3 was slower, heavier, bigger, and far more wieldy than the model it replaced. The ZB handled well, had accurate steering and a more powerful engine. This was the price of a common model covering from a farmer's pick-up van (a 'ute' in Australia), through to family motoring, to a car for sports touring. It was not all bad, as the mid-range Farina cars were excellent family saloons with a massive boot for luggage and the MG and Riley versions were quite fast.

The other problem that BMC fought was the numbers of franchised garages they supplied, where often only one or two makes were covered; for instance, there were Austin garages, Morris and MG garages, Riley garages and Morris and Wolseley garages. An

The 'new' A55 Cambridge ADO9.

Austin garage would not sell a Wolseley, or a Riley or a Morris, so BMC produced mid-range saloons that could be sold at any of them, with the added advantage of the majority of common spares to all models. An A55 front wheel bearing was the same as a Wolseley 15/60 or a Mk3 Magnette, etc. This kept prices down as well. The idea to produce a common shell and running gear paid off. BMC made 900,000 Farina cars under various badges from 1959 through to 1971. The cars became a byword for reliability and strength, with the vast majority of country taxi firms using white-roofed Morris Oxford series 6 models. The taxi version had a very rattly and oily diesel version of the 1,489cc B series engine, producing just 45bhp; top speed was in the low 60s, but fuel consumption was very good.

The MG and Riley versions of the car were set aside by their different styling to the others. The rear fins were cut off at about 30 degrees, improving the rear end of the very angular Pinin-Farina-styled car. When the updated model – the ADO38 – arrived, the Austin, Morris and Wolseley had the rear fins trimmed off, but the MG and Riley bodies remained unchanged. Being able to spot a Mk3 Magnette from a Mk4 Magnette requires a keen eye and mechanical knowledge.

Whilst the floor pan came directly from the Austin Cambridge A55 (I defy you to tell the difference while laying underneath both cars on a garage ramp), the engine and gearbox has a more complex history. There were minor alterations to the chassis/floor to accommodate the larger sharp-edged body, which had been styled by the Italian firm Pinin-Farina. The French Peugeot 404 saloon, also styled by them, looked very similar. On the MG and Riley, the front panel, bonnet, rear wings and grille were styled in-house by BMC stylist

When the body was restyled in 1961, the MG version kept the big rear fins, becoming the Mk4. It was deemed it would cost too much to alter such a small volume of cars.

The Riley also kept the bigger fins, becoming the 4/72.

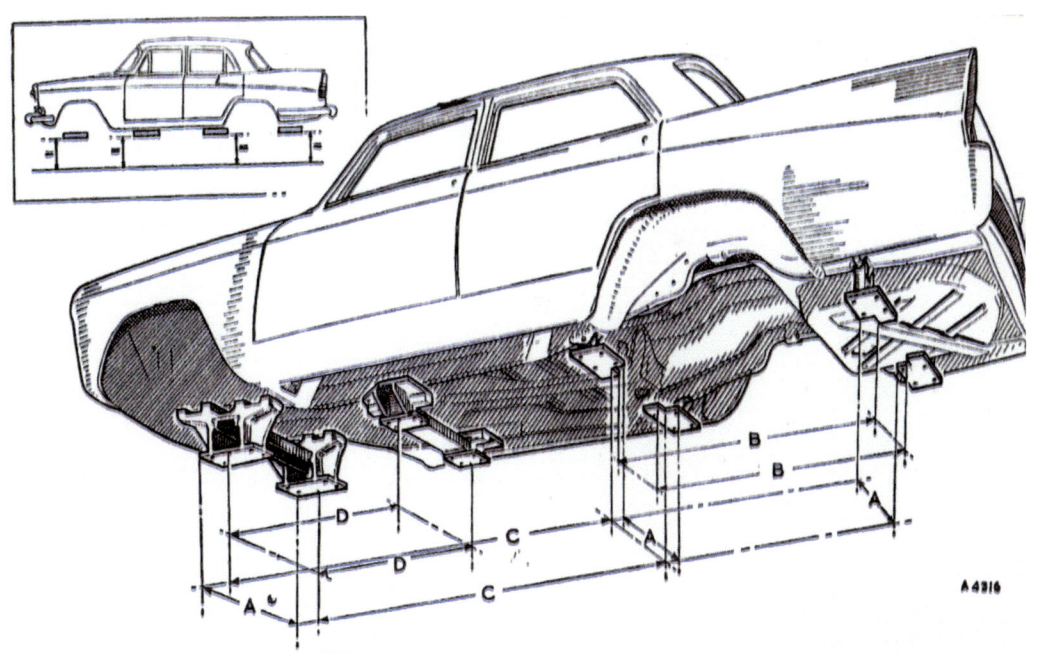

From underneath the early Austin A55 and all the Farina versions were identical. (BMIHT)

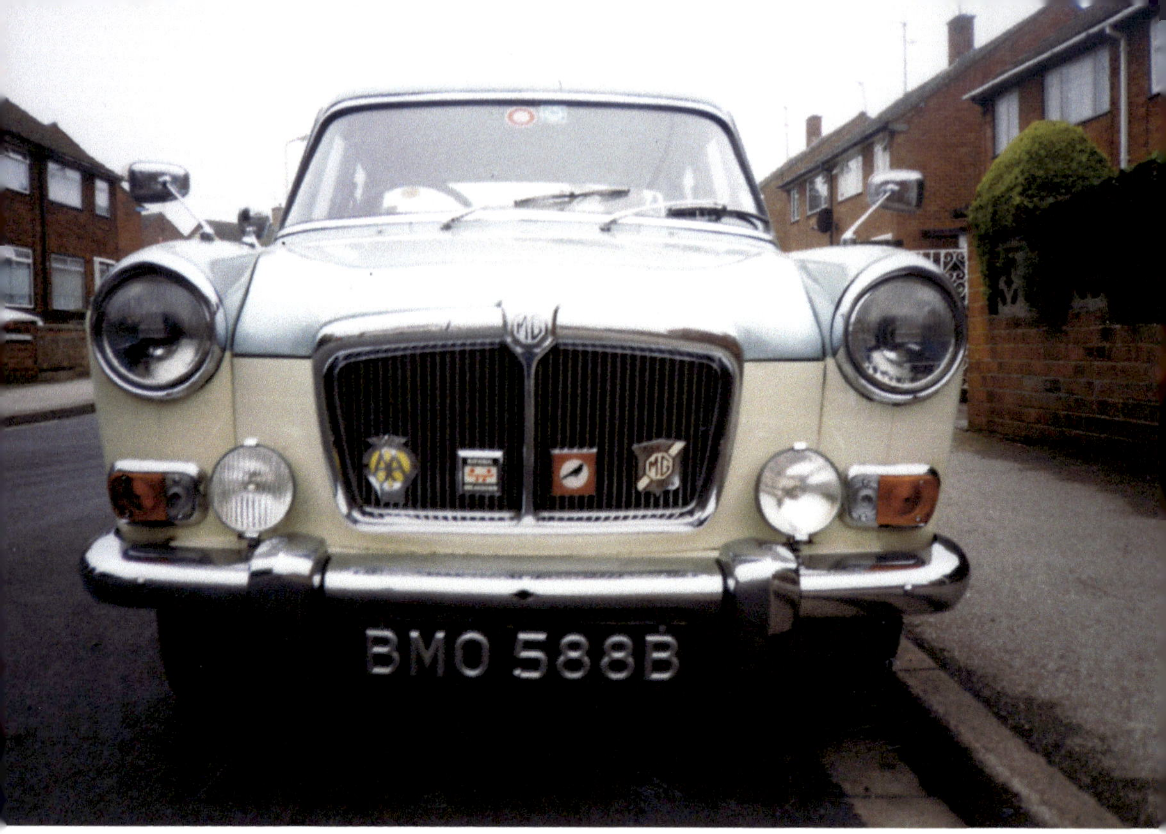

*Above*: BMC stylist Sid Goble successfully added the radiator fronts to suit the various marques.

*Left*: The twin SU HD4 carburettors of the MG and Riley, which were unique to them.

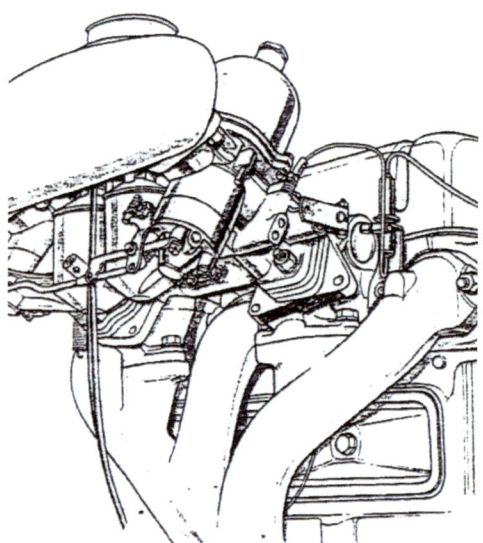

M.G. Magnette Mark III . .

new exhaust manifold provides a freer gas flow and incorp spots. Diaphragm-type S.U. carburettors are now fit

Sid Goble, and very successfully applied to the hull. A change of make simply required a different grille, front panel and bonnet. The engine on the ADO9 was the standard BMC B series, designed in 1950–51 by Bill Appleby of the ADO Engine Design Office. He was assisted by Eric Bareham and Jimmy Rix, who between them had cloned the 1947 Austin A40 Cambridge engine from the four-cylinder 2-litre Austin 16. The 16hp engine was itself developed from the six-cylinder Austin lorry engine, and that devolved from a Vauxhall lorry engine, itself a copy of a 1930s General Motors engine! The three men had developed the smaller 803cc A series the year before, as used in the A30 and Morris Minor series 2, and were now responsible for the B series. The B was not new, however. It had to use the pre-war Austin 12hp engine's crankshaft and cylinder bore centres due to the cost of new machinery, as had the A40 before it. The 1,489cc B series of 1953 had its bores set further apart and was also in production as a 1,200cc, the same size as the previous A40 of 1947. The engine went first into an MG, the 1953 MG Magnette Z series, later called a ZA. It was also fitted to all the Austin, Morris, and Wolseley saloon cars, and smaller commercial vehicles. The unit put into the Mk4 MG Magnette and the Riley 4/68 was that of the early MGA 1500 (68bhp) and the later MG ZB. On the Mk3 Magnette there was no camshaft drive for the tachometer, but there was on the Riley 4/68, as there was on the MGA. This 1,489cc engine produced 68bhp on paper, but 66bhp on a brake. The 1959 Farina's engine produced 2bhp less than the previous ZB. The only difference was the use of SU HD4 carburettors with a rubber diaphragm for the choke, as used in larger form on Jaguars, big Rovers, and Rolls-Royce/Bentley cars (BMC owned the SU company).

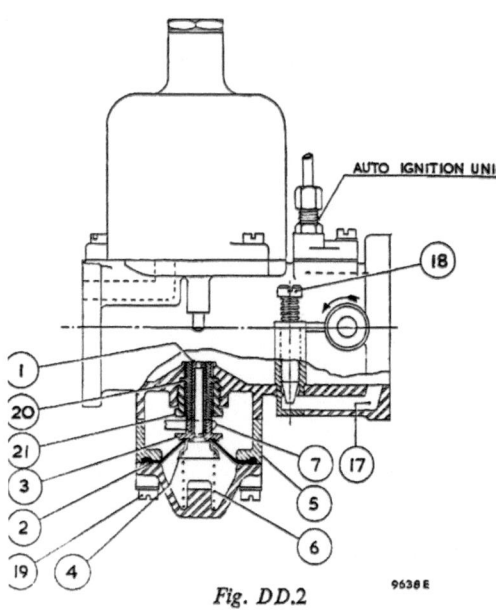

Fig. DD.2

1. Jet.
2. Diaphragm.
3. Jet cup.
4. Jet return spring cup.
5. Diaphragm casing.
6. Jet return spring.
7. Jet actuating lever.
17. Mixture passage.
18. 'Slow-run' valve.
19. Float-chamber securing screw.
20. Jet bearing.
21. Jet screw.

Diagrammatic view of the HD4 with its unusual rubber diaphragm. (BMIHT)

The 1960 MG Mk3 Magnette chassis 13782. (Mike Collins)

The gearbox was of standard BMC type, with no synchromesh on the lowest gears. The synchromesh on second to third was very weak and often gave up after 10,000 miles. Farina owners are often good at double de-clutching. The rear axle was the standard banjo BMC type of 4.3 to 1 ratio.

The car was revamped in 1962 and became the Mk4 MG Magnette and Riley 4/72. The engine had grown to 1,622cc from the MGA 1600 Mk2, but the car kept the SU HD4 carburettors that only it ever used and power was up to 72bhp – that of the last MGA 1500. BMC took the time to ask MG what they would do to improve the car's bad name for steering and handling. The worm-and-peg steering was very vague, with quite a bit of play even when new. What the car wanted was the MGB's rack-and-pinion steering, but this would have meant too much re-engineering. As such, the model ended up with an anti-roll bar fitted front and rear, the car being lowered by an inch all round, the wheel track widened, and the rear axle moved along the spring an inch rearwards to lengthen the wheelbase. The dampers were uprated to Armstrong double-acting lever-arm type and the rear spring rate changed. With a set of radial ply tyres, the car was now quite presentable. The cable-driven tachometer of the Riley was deleted in 1966 and the MGB/Midget/Marina 1.8 electronic had one fitted – one that counted the pulses of the ignition points. Both engines fitted into the MG and Riley were then identical.

The interiors were of leather-faced seats, and the only real change to the interior specification was to the rear seats. The Mk3 Magnette had individual seats whereas the

*Above*: The 1967 MG Mk4 Magnette chassis 30401 (a very rare automatic) six years apart, showing an average of just 2,200 sold each year. (Andrew Brock)

*Right*: A Riley 4/72 with an anti-roll bar on the front suspension, which was a big improvement to the car's handling. Note the multitude of ball joints – six in total.

Double-acting front damper of the later cars – again, improving the ride.

Riley had one rear bench seat. The early cars used modified ZB front seats, but in mid-1959 it used those from the Wolseley 15/60 (trimmed in leather with rounded corners) and at the same time the MG gained the Riley rear bench seat. This was to cut costs.

What was basically an Austin A55 frame had a restyled skin by the Italian Pinin-Farina to sharpen it up, then it had various radiator grilles added. The MG purists were very upset by the 'breeding counts' advert, where the new Mk3 Magnette was said to owe its design to the racing MG K3 Magnette. This simply was not true (see page 5).

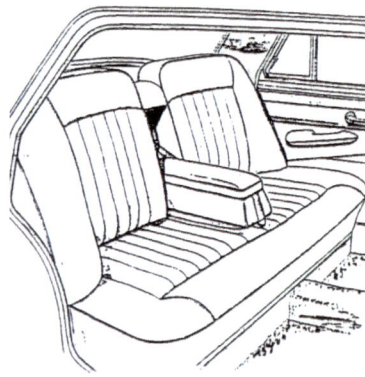

Deep rolls at the edges of cushion and squabs ensure good or rear-seat passengers. There is a central folding armrest, in ( to a small padded armrest on each door

**M.G. Magnette Mark III . . .**

*Left*: Original rear seats of the Mk3 were very good – individual buckets almost. (*Autocar*, 1959)

*Below*: Mk4 seats were the same as the Riley 4/68-4/72.

The Riley 4/68 ran from 3 February 1959 to 4 October 1961; the Riley 4/72 from 19 September 1961 to 24 October 1969; the Mk3 Magnette from 12 November 1958 to 4 January 1961; and the Mk4 Magnette from 18 September 1961 to 8 April 1968. The Morris Oxford s6 and Wolseley 16/60 continued until 1971. The Morris Oxford was very popular as a taxi.

*Right*: The Riley dashboard very well fitted out and included a tachomete (cable driven on the 4/68 but electronic on the 4/72).

*Below*: MG dashboard using some of the Z series instruments.

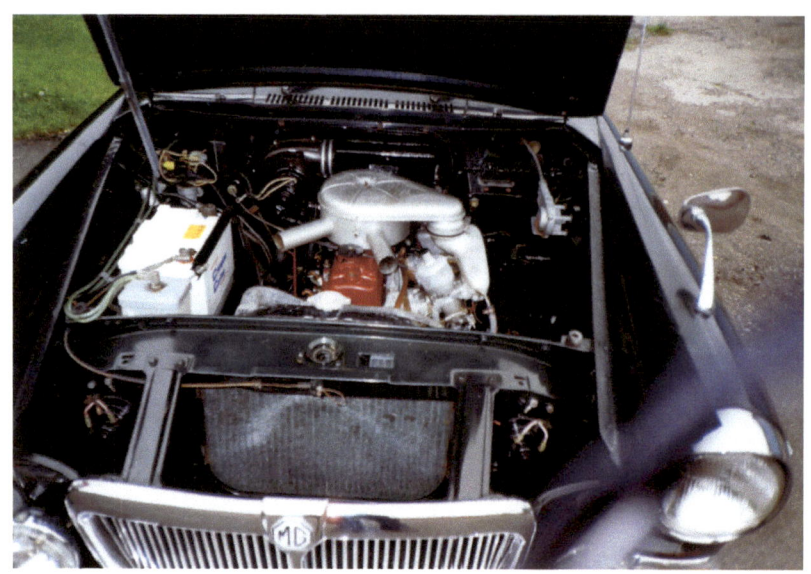

The engine bay was identical for both the MG and Riley models. (Malcolm Chapman)

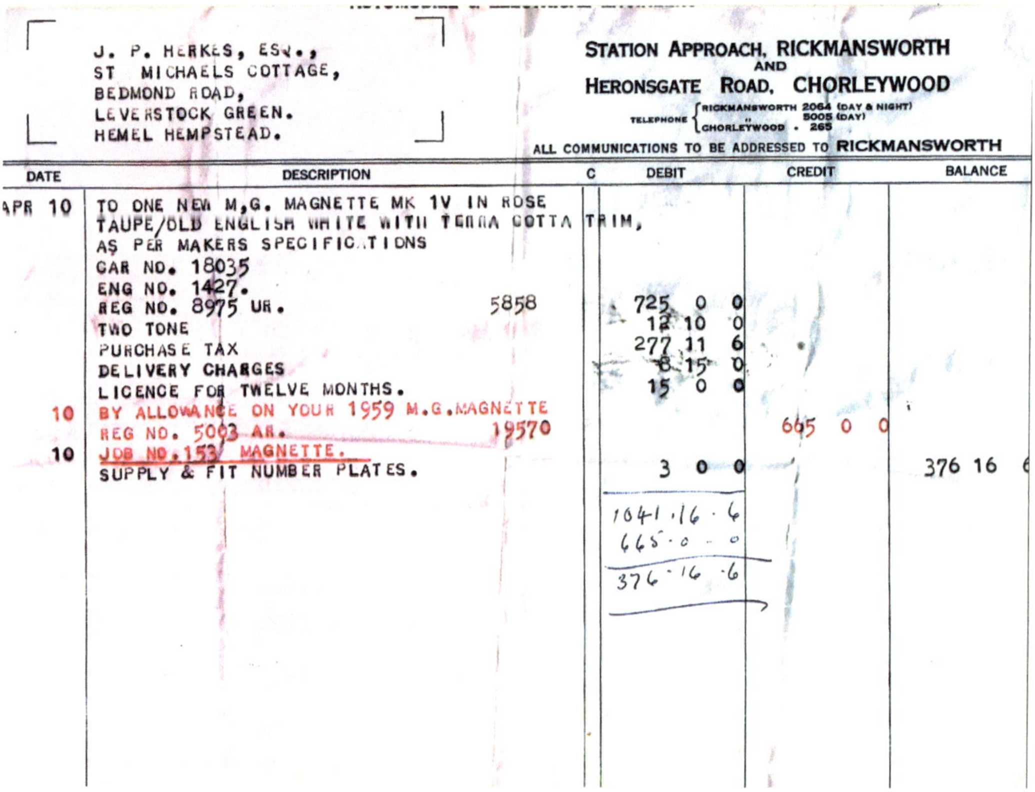

J. P. HERKES, ESQ.,
ST MICHAELS COTTAGE,
BEDMOND ROAD,
LEVERSTOCK GREEN.
HEMEL HEMPSTEAD.

STATION APPROACH, RICKMANSWORTH
AND
HERONSGATE ROAD, CHORLEYWOOD
TELEPHONE RICKMANSWORTH 2064 (DAY & NIGHT) " 5005 (DAY) CHORLEYWOOD . 265
ALL COMMUNICATIONS TO BE ADDRESSED TO RICKMANSWORTH

| DATE | DESCRIPTION | C | DEBIT | CREDIT | BALANCE |
|---|---|---|---|---|---|
| APR 10 | TO ONE NEW M.G. MAGNETTE MK 1V IN ROSE TAUPE/OLD ENGLISH WHITE WITH TERRA COTTA TRIM, | | | | |
| | AS PER MAKERS SPECIFICATIONS | | | | |
| | CAR NO. 18035 | | | | |
| | ENG NO. 1427. | | | | |
| | REG NO. 8975 UR. 5858 | | 725 0 0 | | |
| | TWO TONE | | 12 10 0 | | |
| | PURCHASE TAX | | 277 11 6 | | |
| | DELIVERY CHARGES | | 8 15 0 | | |
| | LICENCE FOR TWELVE MONTHS. | | 15 0 0 | | |
| 10 | BY ALLOWANCE ON YOUR 1959 M.G.MAGNETTE | | | | |
| | REG NO. 5003 AR. 19570 | | | 665 0 0 | |
| 10 | JOB NO.153 MAGNETTE. | | | | |
| | SUPPLY & FIT NUMBER PLATES. | | 3 0 0 | | 376 16 6 |
| | | | 1041.16.6 | | |
| | | | 665.0.0 | | |
| | | | 376.16.6 | | |

A receipt for a new Mk3 Magnette where Mr Herkes has traded in his ZB Varitone Magnette. A number of MG enthusiasts who did this went back and demanded their old car back!

# 2
# Selling the Cars

In the days of BMC virtually every town of any size had its Austin or Morris dealer. Average earnings were between £12 and £17 a week for the working man, but the MG and Riley Farina were aimed at the lower end of middle managers with families. They perhaps took home £100 to £130 a month, so the car was about a year's salary to them – not so different to today. *Motor* magazine quotes the price of a Mk3 as £1,012 inclusive of purchase tax (replaced years later by VAT). The Riley 4/68 was £1,028 whereas the Wolseley 15/60 was £991. The Morris and Austin versions for 1959 were £858.

The Farina range were one of the last cars made in the UK to still have a starting handle.

*Above*: The Farina MG alongside its small companion, the MG 1100/1300, which outsold it many times over. (Doug Green)

*Left*: The publicity department worked hard to sell the cars.

The running costs were much higher if you were not mechanically minded and had to use a garage for servicing. The cars needed greasing at least every 3,000 miles. Other services were at 6,000- and 12,000-mile intervals. Whilst waiting for the car to be serviced you could choose from the optional extras your dealer wanted to sell you.

The writers of the adverts for the Farina MG were really on the edge of what today would be deemed 'fake news'. Those for the Riley version was more truthful, calling the 4/68 and 4/72 'Gentlemen's Cars' – fast touring vehicles of some comfort. The Mk3 and Mk4 adverts were trying to say things the car simply was not. 'Breeding counts' one says, though the car is a direct descendant of the Austin line of A40-A50-A55 and shares the body of the A60. 'The car that recaptures the desire to drive' says another. The numerous steering ball joints and a worm-and-peg steering box all adding up to at least 2 inches of free play at the steering wheel rim bears no comparison to the accurate rack and pinion of almost all the other post-war MGs. The advert that today would get the company into court with the Advertising Standards Authority (ASA) is: 'Completely new with a flawless sporting pedigree,' which appeared in 1959 for the Mk3 Magnette. What races had an Austin A50 or A55 Mk1 or A55 Mk2 Farina ever won? The Mk4 was also available with automatic transmission, which stole quite a bit of the engine's power, so it was not a fast car at all. But it was easy to drive and later the MGB shared the same automatic gearbox. The MGB, however, had over 90bhp and 1,800cc, plus it was also a lot lighter. 1,699 Mk4s left the factory as automatics out of a total of 14,356 between 1961 and 1968. Very few survive today.

All the motoring press were carrying adverts for these medium range BMC saloons, but they were up against the Ford Cortina.

# Travel 1st Class

Riley make cars for people who want 1st class travel — and won't settle for less. Consider the Riley 4/Seventy Two. A luxury car if ever there was one. Sleek, distinguished, craftsman-finished.

Step into its spaciousness. Relax into the softness of real leather upholstery. See satin-smooth polished walnut before you, feel sumptuous deep pile carpet beneath your feet.

Then switch on. Feel the full-blooded throb of power — twin carb. power that responds to your touch, takes you smoothly through traffic, builds up speed without strain.

Add the pleasures of effortless fast-cruising with fully automatic drive, the economy of touring at an admirable 35 m.p.g. — you have all that makes for 1st class travel with a Riley 4/Seventy Two.

 Get in touch with your Riley dealer today and take the 4/Seventy Two on a trial run.

BY BRITISH RILEY

The Riley dashboard was much better laid out.

As I have said before, the car was indeed a very capable family saloon that seated five. It was a robust car with a truly massive boot for luggage. I ran a 1963 Mk4 for almost ten years and it only let me down once – a broken top leaf on a rear spring.

The Farina Magnettes were up against very stiff opposition and perhaps trespassing into an area they were not really suited for. Vauxhall's VX4/90 was faster and Ford's Cortina GT and 1600E were much better value, as well as faster. Rootes' Sunbeam Rapier, with its sculptured styling by Loewy, looked much smaller when compared with the Farina's straight lines. The Rapier won many rallies, as did the Fords, but there is no record of a Farina MG winning very much.

# 3
# The Different Models

Not only were there originally seven models of the Farina ADO9 (Austin Design Office), but there were also modifications during production and a redesign of all seven in 1962. This leads to difficulty in identifying what is what. The various models from 1958 to 1961 were:

Austin A55 Mk2 Cambridge saloon
Austin A55 Mk2 Cambridge Countryman estate
Morris Oxford series 5 saloon
Morris Oxford series 5 Traveller estate
Wolseley 15/60 saloon
Riley 4/68 saloon
MG Magnette Mk3 saloon

The updating of the models changed their designation to ADO38, and between 1961 and 1971 the nine became:

Austin A60 Cambridge saloon
Austin A60 Cambridge Countryman saloon
Morris Oxford series 6 fleet model saloon
Morris Oxford series 6 deluxe saloon
Morris Oxford series 6 diesel-engine saloon (a popular taxi)
Morris Oxford series 6 Traveller estate
Wolseley 16/60 saloon
Riley 4/72
MG Magnette Mk4 saloon

Note the cheap version of the Oxford for fleet users and the diesel version, which were often used as taxis. The deluxe had a white roof.

Of the two makes this book is concerned with, it is the MG Magnette that is the enigma. MG made sports cars that were easy to drive, cheap to run, and usually quite small in size. The big Farina ADO9 saloon sat rather odd in the company's line up of

*Above*: A Riley, MG and an Austin A60 at the rear.

*Below*: Wolseley 15/50 with its smaller brother, the Wolseley 1500. It uses the same engine and gearbox, making it a very nippy little car.

models on offer. The car was actually built at Cowley in Oxford, not at Abingdon, and had been a BMC design, but it carried an MG chassis plate with 'MG of Abingdon' on it. The Riley Farina sat far better in the selection, as Riley had always had a well-fitted-out plush saloon in their range. There was the MG Z Magnette, but this was a very different animal to the big Farina MG. The Z was sporting, had excellent handling and looked fast, whereas the Mk3 Magnette was far more of a mini-limousine with very average handling.

It is not hard to clone a Farina as the panels that differ at the front simply unbolt. The fins might cause more problems, but there is a least one Wolseley 16/60 with a Riley 4/72 bonnet, front panel, and grille running about. I once built a Mk3 MG Magnette estate car by putting the relevant panels onto my green 1961 A55 Mk2 Cambridge Countryman. I also used the Mk3's dashboard but put the Austin's round gauges into it (the scrap donor car's octagonal ones had already been removed when I got there). The A55 Mk2 was the equivalent of the Mk3 MG Magnette and shared its 1,489cc engine, producing 55bhp (the A55 only had a single carburettor). I pulled a 14-foot caravan about the Highlands of Scotland as we lived in Forres at the time. Whilst there was an MG badge on the radiator grille, there was and Austin one on the bumper (just visible in the photo). The rear estate car doors still had 'Austin Cambridge' in chrome script. It fooled many people until it was scrapped in 1975 (I sold it to a mate who took it home to South Wales. A slag heap slipped and buried it one night).

All Farinas have a towing eye bolted to the left-hand front bumper mount under the car, as well as a starting handle (one of the last cars to be sold with one).

This car began as a 1961 Austin A55 Mk2 Countryman. I added the MG front end and bonnet and the MG dash. It was all just spanner work. I had put a Morris Oxford grille on it earlier.

The Austin before I swapped the front ends in Morayshire on holiday.

Identifying a Mk3 and Mk4 can be done from the chassis plate (now called a VIN plate – Vehicle Identity Number) under the bonnet. Five letter prefixes indicate the following:

G for MG; R for Riley
H for engine size (1,400–20,00cc)
S for four-door body
No. 1 for Mk3; No. 2 for Mk4
L for left-hand-drive

Dating of the first MG car of that year:

101 – November 1958
166 – January 1959
7978 – January 1960
15123 – January 1961
16776 – last Mk3
16801 – first Mk4 in September 1961
17606 – January 1962
20915 – January 1963

23363 – January 1964
25983 – January 1965
28629 – January 1966
30332 – January 1967
31120 – January 1968
31120 – last Mk4 in April 1968 (31286 – last CKD Mk4 for Eire)

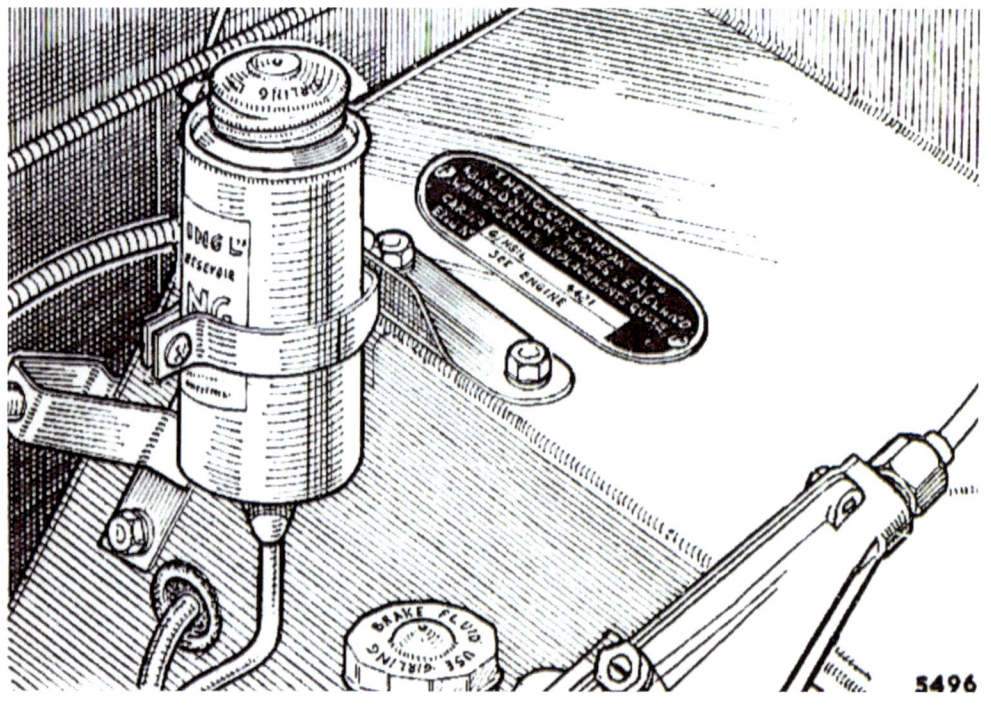

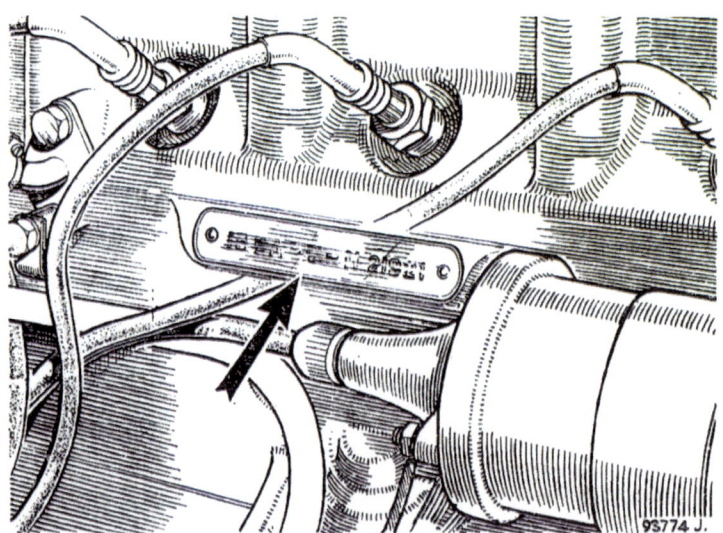

*Above*: The car's data plate on the passenger side (RHD) of the engine dash panel carrying the car number (chassis number). (BMIHT)

*Left*: The engine number is on the nearside of the block by the coil. (BMIHT)

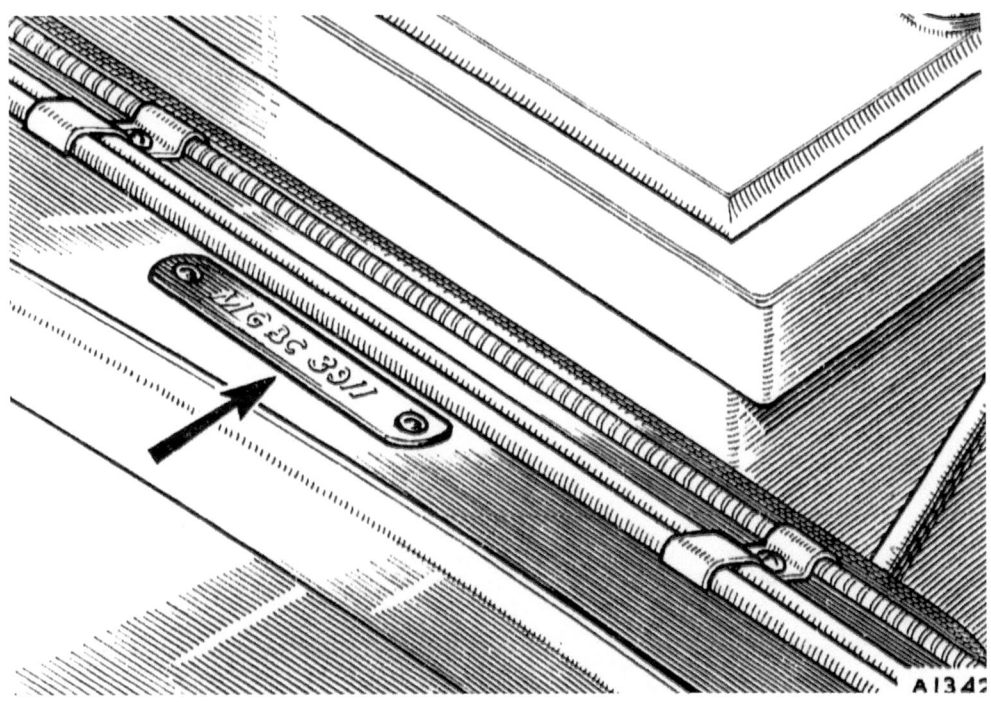

The body number (NOT the same as the car number) is on the offside wing valance. (BMIHT)

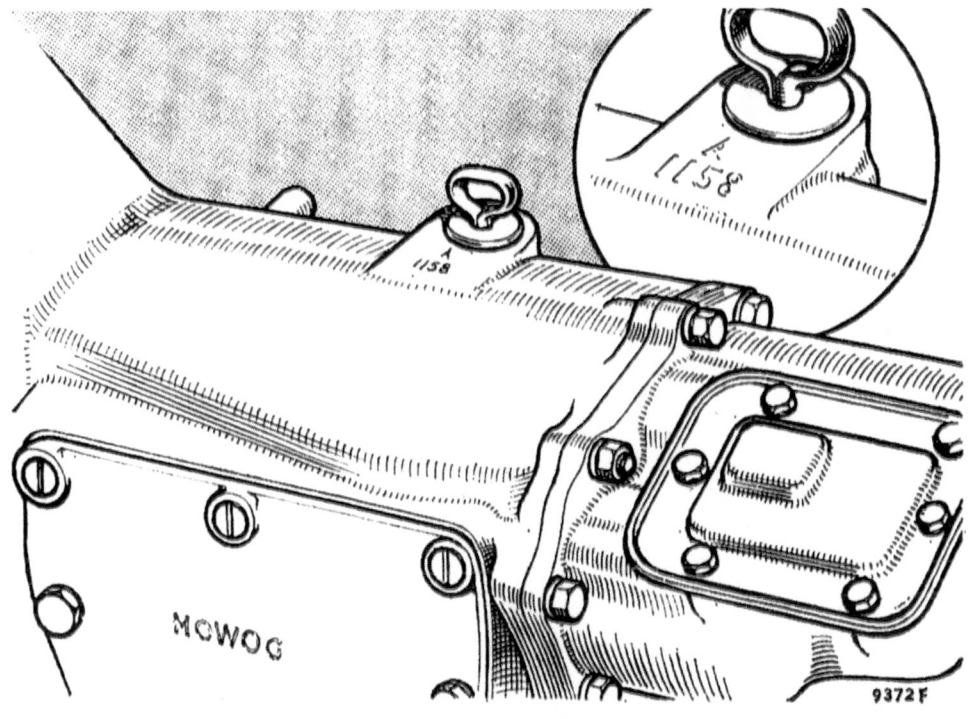

The gearbox number is stamped by the dipstick. (BMIHT)

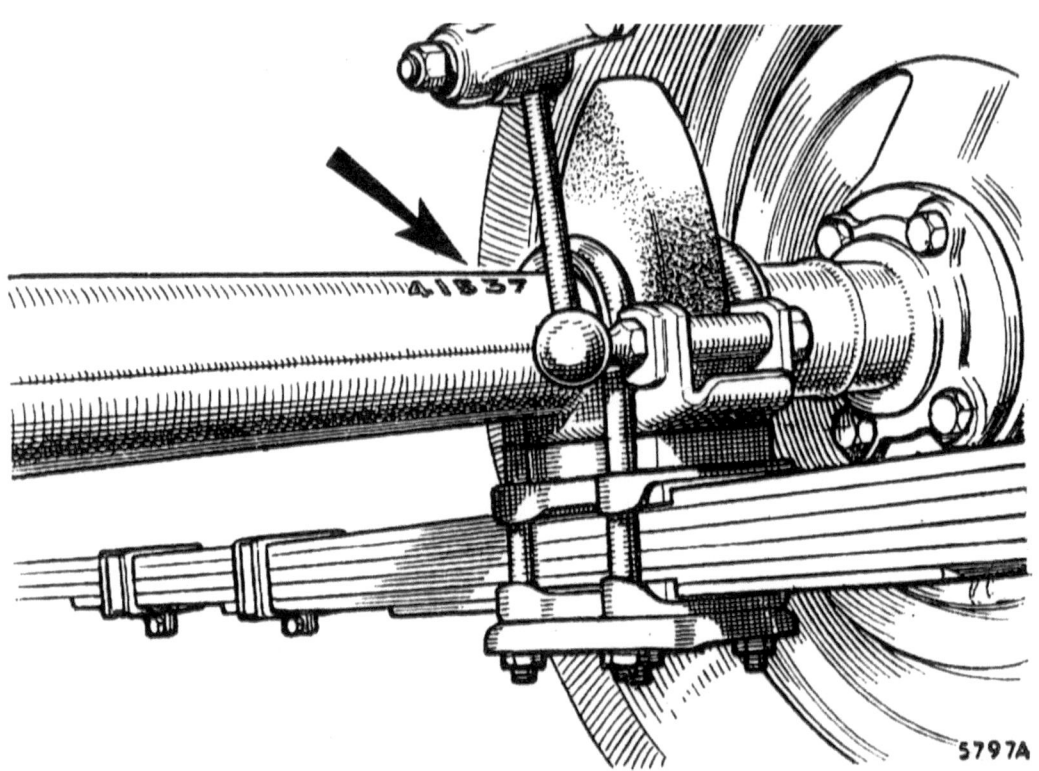

The rear axle number is on the nearside axle tube. (BMIHT)

# 4
# Riley 4/68 and MG Magnette Mk3

The MG Magnette Mk3 was to replace the MG ZB. The Riley 4/68 was to replace an earlier Riley model discontinued some years before – the 1.5-litre RMA. There had been a Riley 1.5 in production since 1956: the little car built onto the Morris Minor floor pan, sharing its body with the Wolseley 1500. This fast little Riley 1.5 was to share its 1,489cc engine and gearbox with the bigger and heavier Farina 4/68.

The MG was the enigma of the Farinas – not too sure what it was meant to be.

Those big Pinin Farina rear fins.

Of the Farina family, the MG Mk3 was to be the sporting family model, whilst the Riley 4/68 was aimed a bit higher at the gentlemen's sports tourer. The dashboard in the Riley was more impressive than that of the MG, which inherited the MG ZB dials. These two cars were the most expensive of the range, the purchase price being nearly a third again over the basic Morris Oxford saloon before tax. Both shared the same bodyshell with its reversed rear fins, giving the cars a much more balanced look compared to the high-pointing spires of the others. The front panel grille, bonnet, dash, front and rear seats, rear fins, and rear lamp units differed from the other Farinas. The front side lamps were shared with the Wolseley, but both bonnets and front panels were uniquely different, even from each other. The Riley had side vents to its grille that wrapped around the lower corners of the front wings. If you look under any Farina bonnet you will see that all the holes are punched for the various models, even the pairs of three holes each side of the radiator on the bonnet shut panel to hold the front panel support bars of the Riley/MG version. Two are for the MG/Riley; the third is for the Wolseley.

The interiors of the MG/Riley used the same front seats after mid-1959. The pleating of the leather ran along the car on the MG, but across the car on the Riley. The early MG Mk3 Magnette had the front seats from the ZB modified to fit the Farina runners. The rear seat on the Riley is a bench type, but 2 inches taller in the backrest than the single-carburettor cars. The Mk3 MG has a very nice rear seat arranged to be two individual seats, with a cut-out portion in the backrest. Both have a central arm at the rear that will fold into the backrest, giving room for an extra passenger. All wearing faces are leather, with the sides in plastic-covered cloth (vynide). By mid-1959, apart from the differing pleating, the MG rear seat was that of the Riley, as were the front seats. Cost cutting had arrived.

Sitting in the cars, the dashboards obviously differ. That of the Riley is all polished wood veneer, whereas the apparently lower polished wood veneer dash of the MG has a black crackle-finish metal face around the instruments. The fixing point of the various dashboards of all the Farinas affix in the same places, so in theory you can easily fit an MG dash to an Austin (as I did). The MG has its ex-MG ZB instruments set in a binnacle in front of the steering wheel, with a larger half-octagonal speedometer. Each side have pairs of small square dials covering water temperature, oil pressure, fuel contents, and an ammeter. The virtually identical switches are haphazard to say the least and take some remembering as to their functions. The Mk3 MG speedometer has a differing TPM number to that of the larger-wheeled ZB. (TPM = Turns-Per-Mile of the speedometer cable, a four-figure number on the dial face.) Whilst the three single-carburettor cars use Smiths gauges, the MG and Riley use Jaeger. This is a bit of a swindle, as the working insides of all the units are the same on all the Farinas and only the shape of the case differs.

The Riley 4/68 dash is more imposing as it sits higher and has large round dial faces. These cover the same information as that in the MG and are set in front of the driver. The two large dials are the speedometer and the cable-driven tachometer, shared with the MGA and Riley 1.5. The cable runs off a bevel gear on the rear of the engine's camshaft – identical to the MGA. The MG has no tachometer, nor even a drive for one. Both cars have 12-volt clocks that are polarity sensitive. Deep pile carpets, a heater and windscreen demister,

Farina styling was very regal.

*Above*: The rear was very imposing.

*Below*: The two-tone sets the car off well.

plus lots of sound-deadening material are standard fitting. The electric motor-driven windscreen wipers are only single speed, but do self-park. There is an indicator stalk on the steering column cowl and a blanking plate where the ignition switch is on the Morris and Austin version. The ignition switch is in the dash on the MG, Riley and Wolseley as there were no steering locks on cars yet.

The steering wheel is huge and set very high (lowered an inch later). It is a typical jukebox style with a huge chrome horn half-ring in its centre. At the horn ring centre is a badge for the various makes. Even when new there is about 2 inches of play at the steering wheel rim. The worm-and-peg steering spiral gear in the steering box is ground in a helix that changes ratio as you steer. Towards full lock the ratio is high, giving more wheel movement on the road, but straight ahead the gearing is lower, requiring more steering wheel movement for a similar correction. There is an adjustment on the steering box for wear. An extreme-pressure (EP) gear oil must be used in the steering box and its idler.

The interiors of the Austin and Morris appear spartan in comparison. The Austin, Morris, and Wolseley share the same dash gauges in different layouts. The Austin A55 Mk2 and Morris Oxford series 5 could be had with steering column change as an option. This was more common on export models. The Austin A55 previous model had column change and a gearbox with an overdrive if required. This was not an option on the Farinas for unknown reasons. Only the column change gearbox had ever been fitted with an overdrive unit. The Morris had a bench front seat, the Austin a split bench front seat.

The body trim was in stainless steel and hub caps had the marque logo centrally, either 'RILEY' or 'MG'. The logo was a Mazak casting affixed to the hub cap, while those of the other were just stamped in. The Mk3 MG shared its hub caps with the MGA, Z series Magnettes, the YB saloon and the TD-TF sports cars. The Riley and MG Farinas were sold with laminated windscreens, whereas the others simply had toughened glass. Both MG and Riley had full-length chromed brass strips down their body waistline and across the boot lid's rear end. There was a reversing lamp fitted to the boot lid centre in chromed cast Mazak. (Mazak is an aluminium, zinc, copper, and magnesium alloy that is used in die casting. It is cheap and requires little finishing before it can be flash-chromed. Eventually, the magnesium corrodes and bursts through the chrome as a white powder. In the USA it is called Zamak.) This centre also hid the boot lid opening handle. In the centre of the rear doors on both models, just in front of the door handles, there was a chromed flash, which was the dividing line of those cars sold with two-tone paint colours. Early cars had the boot lid, rear fin tops and the roof in one colour, while the doors, bonnet and front wings were another. This later became simplified as the full-length waist strip was the colour divider.

This early Mk3 colour scheme followed that of the Austin A55 Mk2 Farina. The two-tone finish was £16 extra. It made the cars look very smart, but as they aged it accentuated the sagging rear springs of the pre-1962 models, making them look tail heavy. (This could be cured by adding an extra top leaf to the springs, as the estate versions had. If you were rich, fitting new estate car springs cured this fault.) It is worth remembering that the MG and Riley Farinas continued using the early bumper over-riders after 1962. Front and rear differ, as do the later Austin A60 types, giving four versions of similar-looking parts. Estate cars used the early rear over-riders till the end as well as the Riley and MG. Estate car rear bumpers also fit the MG and Riley. The estate cars are today very rare indeed, few have survived.

Big doors and a high-set steering wheel. They were big because few cars in those days had no power steering.

As well as the body hull, the front suspension, steering, gearbox, brakes and rear axle were all standard BMC units. There were no anti-roll bars on the early cars. This was odd as the A55 Cambridge (which had the same floor pan as the Farina) had carried a rear anti-roll bar as it was known to be tail heavy. The rear axle ratio of the twin-carburettor cars was higher than the others to take advantage of the more powerful engine. On the MG and Riley it was 4.3 to 1, the single-carburettor cars were 4.55 to 1, and the estate cars 4.875 to 1.

The basic models had the standard 55bhp BMC B series engine, as fitted to a huge number of BMC's cars and vans. These all had one SU HS4 fitted, even the Austin Farina engine. Austin had, until 1958, used down-draught Zenith carburettors. The engine used in the MG Mk3 was basically that of the MG ZB saloon, and the one in the Riley 4/68 was the pre-1956 MGA 1500 (still in use in the Riley 1.5 when the 4/68 arrived). Both the Mk3 and 4/68 had twin SU HD4 carburettors, which are peculiar to only these two Farina models, not being used anywhere else. In much larger sizes the SU HD was used on the big saloons of Jaguar, Rolls-Royce, Bentley and Rover. Today it can be hard to find spares, as the jet control and choke are a rubber diaphragm and not the usual spring-loaded brass jet tube.

The engine turned out 66bhp, two less than the ZB, Riley 1.5 and pre-1956 MGA 1500. The '68' part of the Riley's model name was supposed to mean 68bhp.

Whilst many think the Farinas all had the same engines, this is not true. Though the single-carburettor cars did use identical units, those fitted to the MG and Riley had harder lead-indium metal in the big end and main bearing shells. Oil pressure was 75psi – 25 higher than the others at 50psi. The cylinder head had bigger ports and bigger valves, with double-valve springs; the camshaft had different valve timing and a different timing curve in the distributor. The two carburettors were silenced by a huge oil bath silencer/filter. The others used paper elements. The exhaust manifold was freer flowing and originally the exhaust pipe was one-eighth of an inch bigger. This led to 12bhp more than the other cars and was basically the current 72bhp MGA 1500 engine with a softer camshaft. 66bhp with an 83lb torque was not a lot to pull around a 2,740lb car. The car did still have a starting handle as standard equipment, which was very useful for timing the engine and setting points and valve gaps, and starting it when the battery was low.

On the family car side, the spare wheel was underneath the car in a tray under the boot, which was wound down using the starting handle. The boot was huge and easy to load as its lid went right down to the bumper height, unlike modern cars where you need to lift the thing up to 3 feet to load them. The handbrake lives by the driver's right thigh – ideal to go up a trouser leg if the cable is allowed to not be adjusted and the lever points too high. I had a Farina where when I pulled the handbrake up hard one day, the whole thing ripped out of the floor due to corrosion.

Whilst the rear brakes (Girling) were those of the A55 Cambridge, the front twin leading shoe drum brakes were much wider and shared with the Ford Consul of the same year. Economy was about 28–30mpg – worse if driven fast. Maximum speed was about 80–85mph, 4mph slower than the ZB Magnette, which had smoother air-cheating lines. The biggest fault with the handling is the roll-oversteer, meaning the car leans alarmingly in fast bends and the back end swings out. The steering is too vague to be capable of catching it soon enough, causing the car to roll and drift like a big softly sprung American car.

## Identifying a 4/68 or Mk3 Magnette

To check that your cars is what it is supposed to be, look between the battery and the wing. Stamped into the metal inner-wing will be the chassis number. This was only done until about mid-1961. The body number on the maker's plate on the dash in the engine bay should be prefixed RHS1 for a 4/68, and GHS1 for a Mk3 MG. The Riley 1,489cc engine will have a prefix of 15RB – same as the Riley 1.5. And the Mk3 MG engine should have 15GE. Cars often have ex-single-carburettor engines fitted; these were prefixed 15AMW (meaning Austin-Morris-Wolseley).

By 1961 BMC had taken notice of the motoring press and the criticism of the cars, and made some much needed improvements to the ADO9. This led to the ADO38 versions. ADO9G had been the MG Mk3, and ADO9R the Riley. ADO38G and ADO38R were very different cars, but unfortunately looked virtually identical to the earlier ADO9.

5

# MG Magnette Mk4 and Riley 4/72

Apart from the differing colour schemes of the Mk3 and Mk4 Magnettes, the majority of people would not give them a second glance, assuming they were the same model but different years. A quick way to check is to look at the front door's rear edge, just above the handle. On the Mk3 there is a small bit of metal riveted to the 'B' post to fill in the window line to the rear door. On the Mk4 the front doors have been modified to carry on the line in the outer panel, so there is no need for the fillet.

No script on the boot lid to differentiate between Mk3 and Mk4. The Riley 4/68 and 4/72 did have that data there.

*Above*: The MG's wooden dash with a radio/cassette of the 1990s.

*Right*: How the spare wheel tray under the boot was lowered by using the starting handle. (BMIHT)

By 1961, UK drivers of 1950s family saloons and some sports cars were blowing up their engines on the new M1 motorway. These 1950s engines were not made for long high-speed running that an extended straight road demanded. Like other manufacturers, BMC took a look at their engines and improved them. The 1,489cc B series was redesigned into an odd 1,622cc size, but strengthened right through. It first went into the MGA 1600 Mk2, giving 90bhp, and then into the Farina cars with 61bhp in single-carburettor form. There was

49

72bhp from the twin carburettors in the MG and Riley. This much-improved engine was longer lasting and more powerful, but perhaps a little rougher running than the 1,489cc version. Second gear synchromesh was improved with harder-wearing cones, but still wore out quite quickly. Torque was up as well, as the single-carburettor cars adopted the 4.3 to 1 rear axle of the MG and Riley. The estate cars now used the 4.55 to 1 ratio.

The Austin, Morris and Wolseley cars had subtle modifications to the high rear fins, dropping them some 2 inches, with restyled rear lamp units. These rear lamp clusters were still individual to type, the Wolseley 16/60 getting a small peak. The stylist tucked the rear bumper in closer to the body so the fins were smaller, and reduced the base car's length by 4 inches to 14 feet 6 inches. As the Riley 4/72 and Mk4 MG Magnette retained their rear fins and bumpers, they remained the older length of 14 feet 10 inches.

The front axle subframe had the lower spring suspension arms and the Armstrong lever damper arms lengthened by 1 inch each. This widened the front track by 2 inches. The rear axle had 1¾ inches added to its width, and the rear axle was moved 1 inch further back along the springs. This lengthened the wheelbase. The rear wheels on an ADO38 are very close to the rear part of the inner wheel arch.

Because of the nose-up attitude of the ADO9, the ADO38 front springs had their spring pan lowered by a half inch. This dropped the front of the car by 1 inch. The old single-acting lever-arm dampers were replaced by double-acting dampers (identified by the two large hexagonal nuts at their base) and the front and rear axles had anti-roll bars fitted. The steering was not improved; it remained the old Marles worm-and-peg system. If fitted with radial ply tyres, the Mk4 MG and 4/72 are much better driver's cars. The handling was much improved, and the roll-oversteer reduced. The car sat better on the road as well, not looking as top heavy as ADO9. At last, the Mk4 MG Magnette handled almost as well as the ZB it replaced and, at nearly 90mph, was now as fast too.

A modification not too well known was the moving back of the rear seat. Well, not quite, as only the front part of the rear wheel arch had a big dent put into it on the ADO38 – possibly

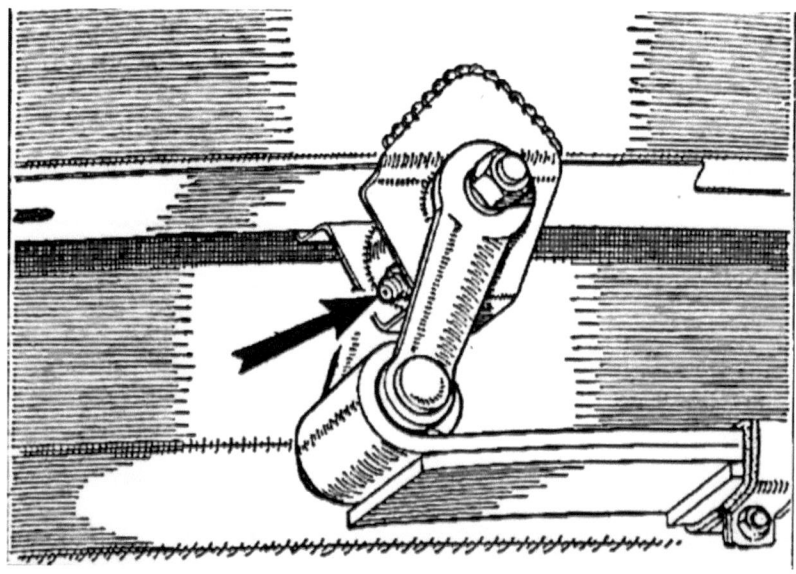

The ancient greased rear shackle of the rear springs on the early cars, later to use silentbloc rubber bushes. (BMIHT)

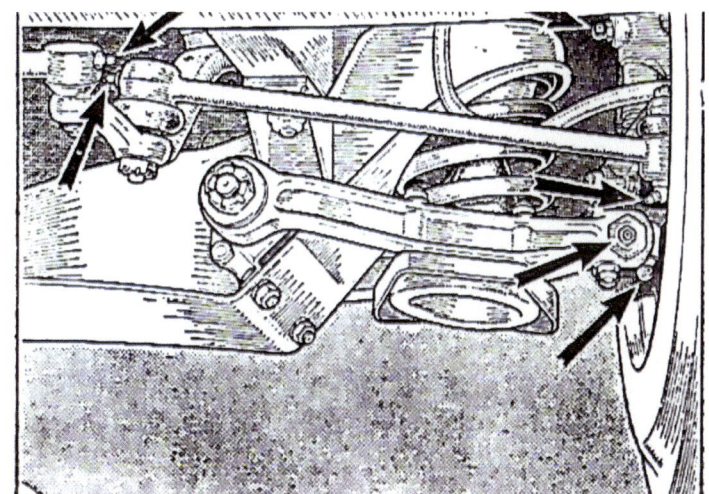

No anti-roll bar on the front suspension of the early cars. (BMIHT)

because the axle was moved rearwards. This permitted the rear seat backrest to sit further back by about 2 inches at the edges, giving more bum room.

Whilst the base cars had rear fin, rear bumper and light changes, the MG and Riley kept the same outer panels. This meant the ADO38 version of the Riley 4/72 and MG Magnette Mk4 were now 4 inches longer than the Austin A60, Morris Oxford series 6 and Wolseley 16/60 versions. The MG and Riley were now much better mannered cars, but the buying public had tarred them with the same brush as the 1959 models. The MGB suffered a similar fate in the MGC version: both looked virtually identical, but one had a 1,789cc four-cylinder engine, while the other a heavy six-cylinder 2,912cc engine. Sales of the single-carburettor cars romped away, but not the sales of the MG and Riley. Both the Riley and MG now were either a single colour all over or had a two-tone colour scheme split at the chrome strip waist line.

The cars had enormous boots that were able to swallow lots of family luggage.

The body numbering of the Riley 4/72 should be prefixed with RHS3 on the chassis plate, located on the dash under the bonnet. No numbers were stamped on the inner wings of these later cars. The MG Magnette Mk4 should read GHS2. The Riley engine should be prefixed 16RA and the MG 16GE. In mid-1966, when the Riley 4/72 went over to the electric impulse-type tachometer, the cable drive was no longer needed. So both the MG and Riley used the same engine, prefixed 16GF, at about Riley number 29,000 and MG 22,000. At about this time the oil pump and sump pressing was standardised with the 1,789cc MGB, which already used the same timing chain and sprockets, with timing cover and rocker cover. The 16GF encompassed these changes as well. The other three makes used a 16AA engine after 1966, previously a 16AMW. The sump change, with its bigger swelling in the cylinder block on these later MGB oil-pump-fitted engines, meant sumps are not interchangeable with earlier engines.

Propeller shafts received sealed-for-life universal joints and the rear spring shackles were fitted with rubber bushes, not bronze bushes. This reduced the number of grease nipples requiring attention every 3,000 miles by four. The rear leaf spring rate and camber was changed to stop the tail-dragging effect of ageing springs. The cooling system was uprated from a pressurised system of 4psi to 7psi. There was still an 82°C thermostat fitted, whereas an 88°C one will improve economy and the heater in the UK.

The maximum speed of the Riley and MG Farina was up to 88–90mph and acceleration was better at 0–50 in 12 seconds – it was previously 13.5. Fuel economy was the same, as the car was the same weight with the same drag coefficient.

The automatic cars were very rare, as the engine was not really powerful enough to cope with the drag of these types of gearbox. The same automatic unit was available for the MGB, but that had 25 per cent more power.

The front side-light and indicator units were peculiar to these models and almost impossible to find today. Their MAZAK cast bodies corroded away quite quickly.

The widening of the rear axle led to improved star splines being used on the longer half-shafts. The 1959–61 cars had square splines. Rear springs now had their centre bolt 1 inch further back, so were not interchangeable with the earlier models and required fitting the right way round. The gearbox also adopted the stronger longer-lasting star splines on its first motion shaft, again requiring the correct star-splined clutch plate.

Because drivers were fitting radial-ply tyres to their cars by 1964, the stresses on the tall steering box were causing the four bolts holding it to the front chassis leg to crack the leg. BMC issued a modification leaflet for retrofitting of a strengthening bracket to the top of the steering box, affixed to the front end of the battery tray. Anyone using radial ply tyres must fit this bracket, but post-1964 cars are already fitted at the factory. To lengthen the life of the steering box, eventually needle rollers were fitted to the cam followers inside the box, as well as the adjustment becoming spring loaded. Again, early box internal parts cannot now be used on later boxes. The later steering boxes have their filler cap at the lower end of the box cover.

Other external changes to the 1961 ADO38 were the fitting of stainless-steel rim bellishers to the ADO38 cars on slightly narrower wheel rims, now 4J and not 4.5J. The exhaust system became the bigger version on all models, but now had both a silencer and expansion box in its length. The parcel tray under the dash gained a crush-edge at its front, to save knees in a crash. All cars now had front seat-belt mountings fitted during manufacture. Original BMC inertia-reel belts relied on the car stopping quickly, as opposed to today's passenger pulling forward quickly. There was only one way to test the older belts: hit something! Modern after-market Securon inertia-reel belts will fit the ADO38 mountings. The front seat adjusters had their locking arrangement improved. Sealed beam headlamp units were fitted and the SU, SP type electric fuel pump fitted. All engines now used the lead/indium bearings, and all models had the laminated windscreens. The BMC Farinas were one of the last cars to still have a starting handle supplied, which was ideal for servicing the engine and winding the car (with the spark plugs removed) out of snow or thick mud.

Not affecting the Riley or MG, BMC did lower the trim standards of the Morris and Wolseley by using Amblar plastic seat coverings and the Morris Oxford becoming available as a fleet model. The deluxe Oxford was identified by its white roof.

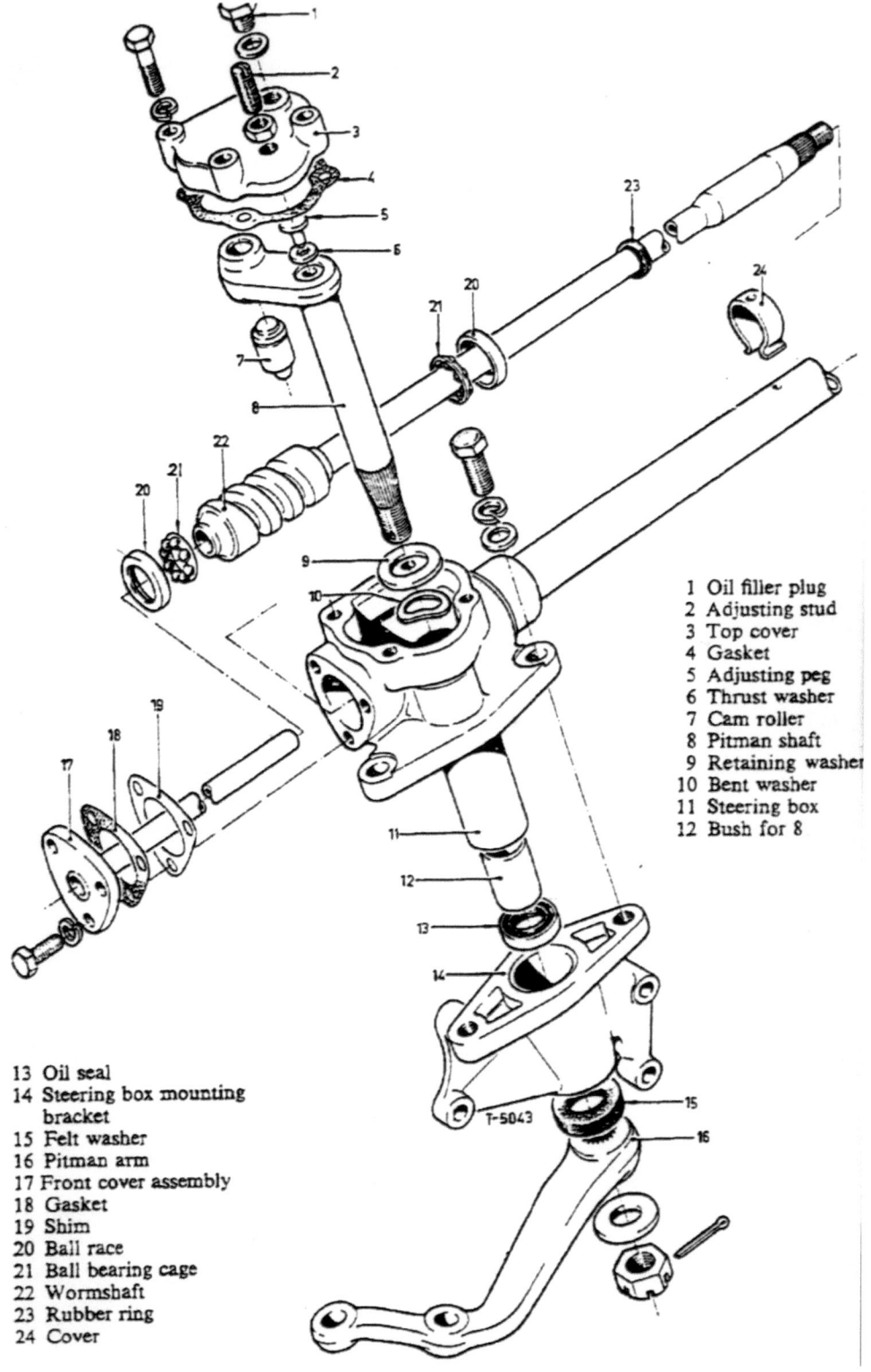

The steering box in an exploded view. (BMIHT)

The steering box in situ.

The steering idler in situ.

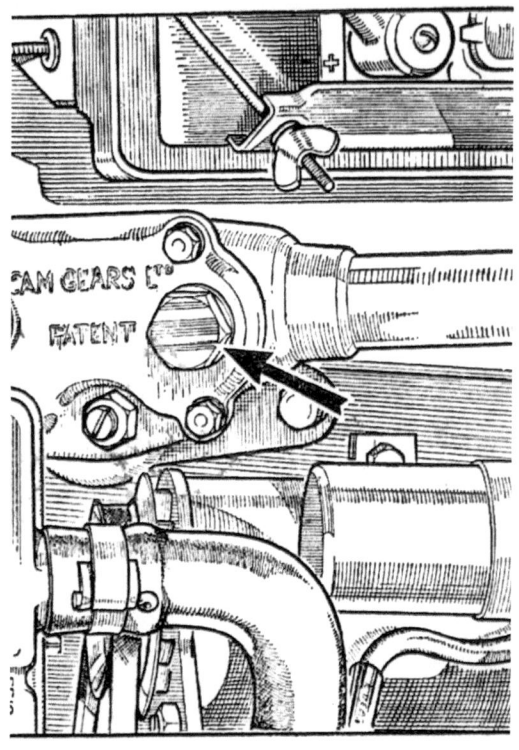

A diagram of the steering box as seen on page 55. (BMIHT)

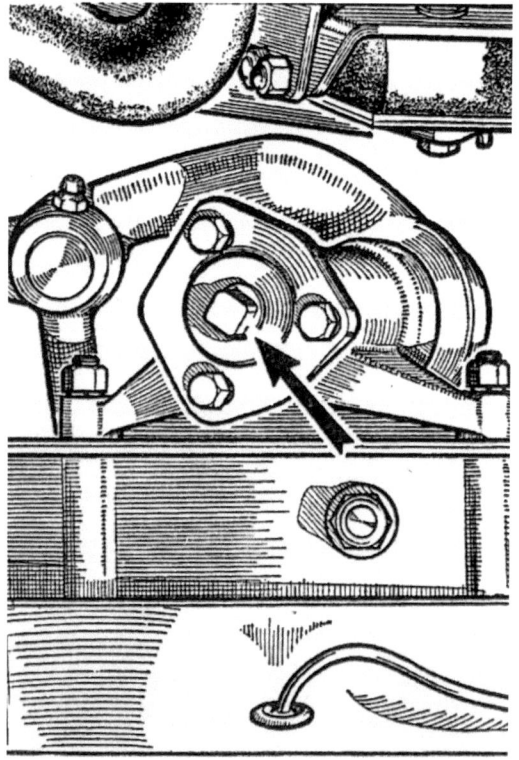

A diagram of the steering idler as seen on page 55. (BMIHT)

*Above*: A New Zealand Riley 4/72 of 1964 with the stainless-steel rim bellishers. (Basil Schewrich)

*Below*: The very first cars had no seat belt mounting, but after 1961 they did. The belts were BMC versions and originally not inertia type.

# 6

# Modifications During Production

*Updates between the Mk3 and Mk4 are quoted in the sections dedicated to them.*

There were quite a number of modifications to the cars during production of a minor nature. Some are very hard to see. One is the changing over from flat rubber blocks to moulded rubber cones on the front suspension subframe. This was again about when ADO38 arrived in late 1961 and renders the interchangeability of the front suspension frame between ADO9 and ADO38 virtually impossible. Another little modification very few know of is the camshaft change early in the life of the 1959 MG and Riley Farina. The timing used was capable of permitting blowback through the carburettors on acceleration, so the key-way that secured the timing sprocket was machined 5° later, retarding the valve timings of both inlet and exhaust valves, curing the fault. The inlet valve had opened at 5° before top-dead-centre (BTDC) now opening at TDC. The 1,489cc engine gained two oil control rings during its life because of high oil consumption, which was acceptable on a sports car but not on a family saloon. The better 1,622cc engine did not suffer as badly.

Because of the poor steering, the whole front suspension subframe was tilted forward by half an inch to alter the castor angle to 3¼° from 1¼°. Longer bolts were needed. The steering wheel was dropped by an inch as well – smaller drivers had been finding themselves looking through it rather than over it. The steering wheel on these older cars have a big diameter to give the necessary leverage to steer. Today we have almost all cars fitted with power-assisted steering. A Farina will develop your arm muscles for you, especially if radial ply tyres are fitted!

The ADO38 1,622cc cars could be had as an automatic, which was not available to the 1,489cc cars. The unit was shared with the new MGB sports car, both using a three-speed Borg-Warner type 35 unit, specially designed for smaller four-cylinder cars. Soon afterwards, there was a similar unit for the little 998cc Mini with four speeds.

The gearbox was modified on the Mk3 at engine number 15GE-U-H15262 to stop the car jumping out of third gear (detent ball location made deeper).

From engine number 16GE-U-H-2544 MG and 16RA-U-H-2936, they were fitted with automatic gearboxes and have a thicker flexiplate for the torque converter. The new plate is 14swg, part number 12H 897. The thinner one was cracking around the bolt holes.

From engine number 16GF-U-H-3190 on both the MG and Riley the gearbox layshaft diameter was increased to that of the Austin half-ton van and diesel cars. The old shaft is 22H 147; the new one 22H 532.

The rear axle was moved 1 inch rearwards on its springs to lengthen the wheelbase on the Mk4, along with both a 2-inch wider rear axle and 1-inch longer front suspension wishbone arms. The front lever-arm wishbone dampers arms are also longer, so not interchangeable with the Mk3. This made the track wider, as well as the wheelbase a bit longer. Steering track control arms were also lengthened to suit. The result of the rear axle moving can be seen on a Mk4 as the wheel being much closer to the rear part of the arch. The front was lowered on the Mk4 as well by adding ½-inch spacers between the spring pan and the lower wishbone arms. As this is halfway along the arm the car actually sits 1 inch lower, giving the MG a much better line. The rear springs of the Mk3 are infamous for settling, and those of the Mk4 are stronger and do not settle. From a distance a Mk3 can often be spotted by its tail-low stance.

The rear spring eye gained silent-bloc rubber bushes at each end, ridding the Mk4 of the Mk3's ancient Austin A40-50-55 threaded pins and grease nipples on the rear shackles.

Wheel rims were altered in 1961 from 4.5J to 4J to suit cross-ply tyres of 5.90 by 14 and radial ply 165 by 14. The locking of the front seat adjusters was improved as well. A Lucas SP-type fuel pump was fitted along with sealed-beam headlamps.

Motorway driving at speed forced the use of steel-backed copper lead bearings for the crankshaft. The 1,489cc cars had an extra oil ring fitted to curb oil consumption when driven fast. This was not followed through to the 1,622cc cars.

Whilst the Mk3 had a 4psi cooling system, the Mk4 had a 7psi system. From 1966 all cars had laminated windscreens; only the MG and Riley had these before.

The steering box began to crack its mountings when radial-ply tyres became popular, so an extra bracing was fitted to its top end bolting to the inner wing in October 1964. This is a good modification to do to earlier cars where radials are used. The damage is caused by the tremendous grip the radial tyre has with the car moving very slowly or stationary and forcing the steering wheel round. It causes the steering box to rock slightly on its bolts. The plate is part number 11H 1507 RHD.

A modification worth doing is to obtain a Morris Marina 1.8 front anti-roll bar. It can be adapted to the Mk4 and reduces the car's rolling quite a bit. The anti-roll bar fitted as standard is only about 2cm thick; that on the Marina 1.8 is 3cm. You may need to source some MGB links for the ends.

Whilst not done by BMC, the Austin Healey sports car, the Farina Austin A99 and A110 and equivalent Wolseley 6/99 and 6/110 used disc brakes. As they use virtually the same front suspension as the ADO38, the discs can be fitted. The problem will be finding a donor. If discs are fitted, then a brake servo will be required as well due to the greater effort needed, as well as a bigger master cylinder reservoir.

Because the car was a reskin of the Austin A55, the majority of bedding-in problems had been sorted and the structure was very strong, if prone to mud traps on the under body, which eventually spread corrosion. In old age they were popular with the banger-racing lads.

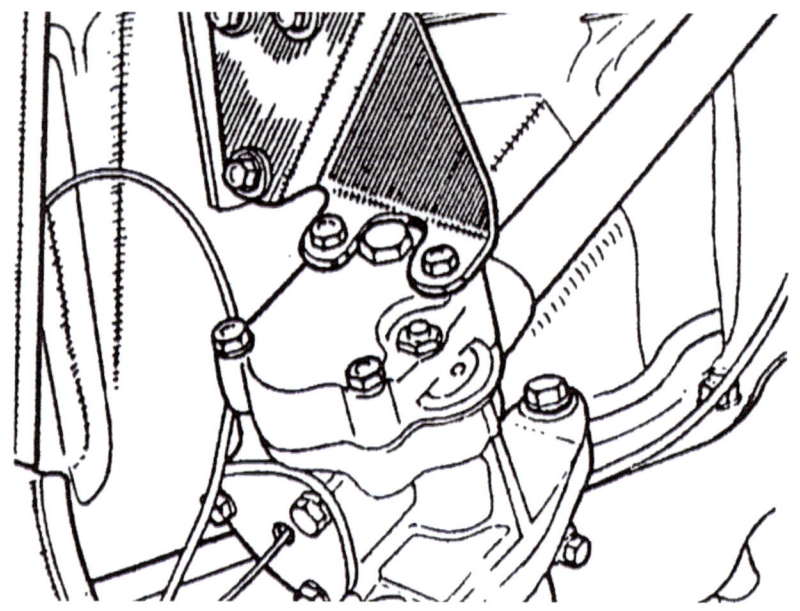

The steering box reinforcing plate as a modification to stop it cracking the sub-frame. (BMIHT)

## THE FRONT SUSPENSION COMPONENTS

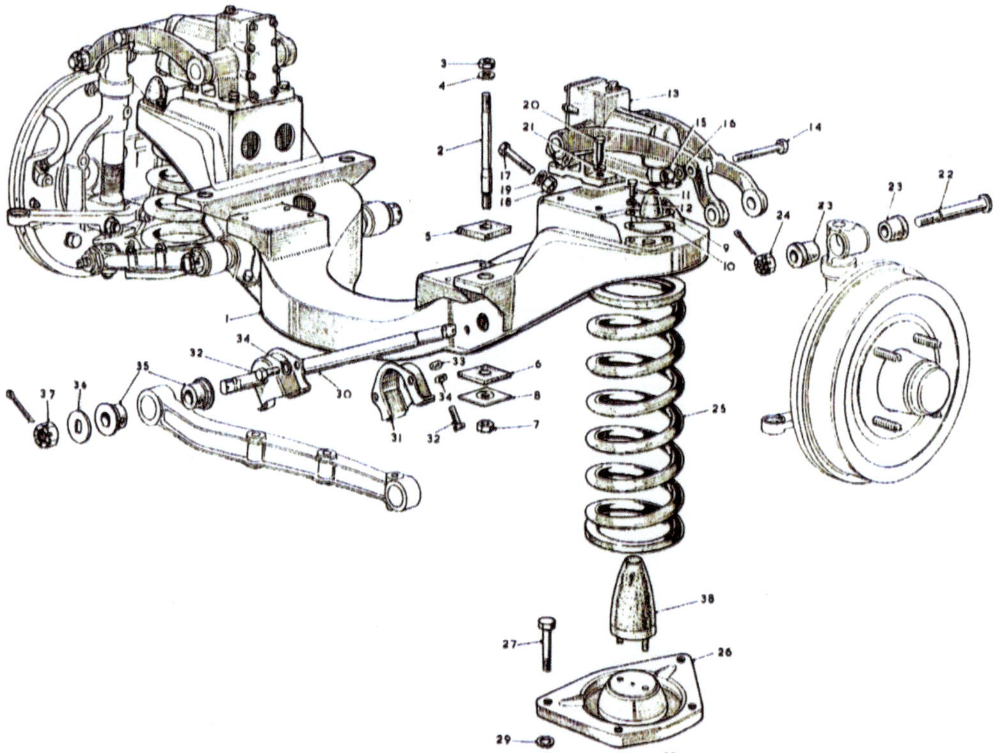

Item No. 5 in the diagram is the early body-mounting pads; later cars used conical ones. (BMIHT)

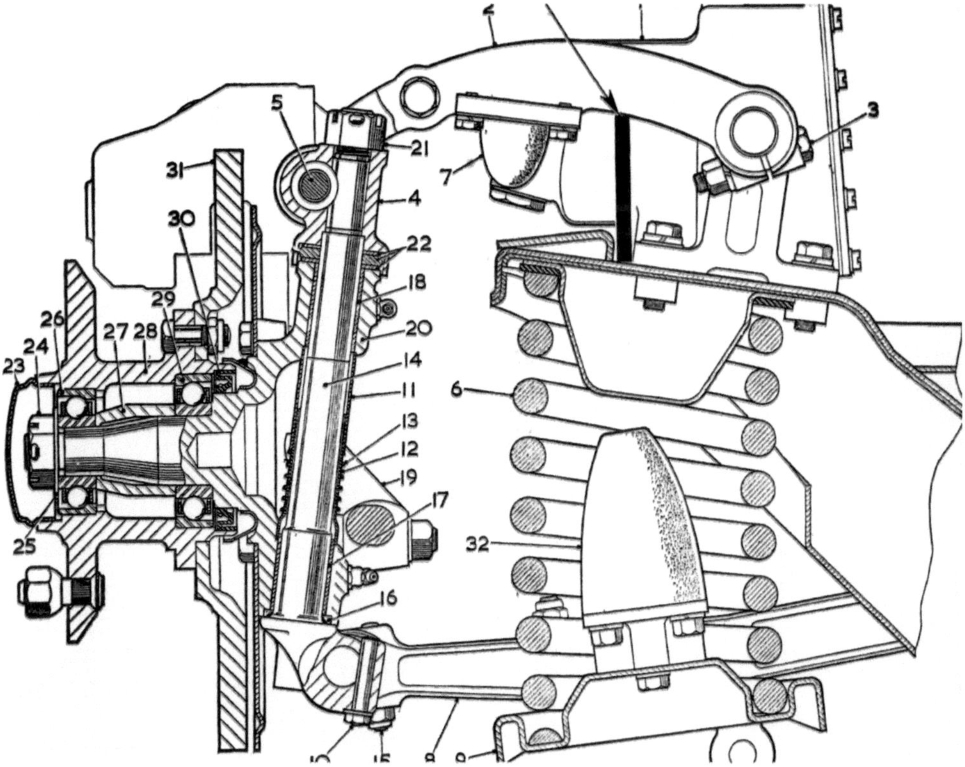

*Above*: A diagram of the Austin Westminster (Wolseley 6/110) disc brakes. (BMIHT)

*Right*: The Farina MG and Riley king pin arrangement, almost identical to those on page 60. (BMHIT)

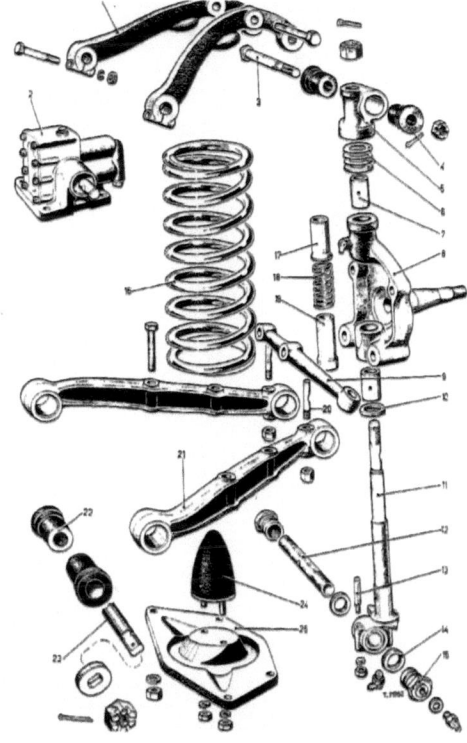

7

# The BMC B Series Engine

The BMC B series was used for many years in a huge number of vehicles. By now any of them might be fitted to your MG. A full list is given so you may trace the unit possibly fitted to your car.

The BMC Austin designed 1,489cc B series engine was first seen in an MG in October 1953. It was shown at the 1953 Motor Show and caused a bit of a rumpus among some who called themselves enthusiasts. The model was the air-smooth MG Z Magnette saloon car. It replaced the Y type with its Morris-based 1,250cc XPAG engine, an engine the company's Wolseley 4/44 would still be using three years later – until 1956.

The source of the B series goes a lot further back in motoring history, as does its younger sibling, the A series, both being born from a 1,200cc OHV Austin engine of 1947. This 1,200cc unit was one of a pair that Bill Appleby, Eric Bareham, and Jimmy Rix at the ADO (Austin Design Office) are supposed to have cribbed from a lorry engine. The original unit was in fact an OHV six-cylinder Chevrolet engine that Vauxhall were building to fit in their pre-war Bedford lorry. It was very successful, and Austin got hold of an example and made his own slightly altered version. It was also very successful, so the Engine Design Department cloned it into two smaller four-cylinder versions for use in the cars. One was a 2,199cc 16hp engine used in the post-war 1945 Austin Sixteen saloon, 25cwt van, and early A90 Atlantic. It was bored out to 2,660cc in the later A90 Atlantic, Austin Taxi, the Champ, and Austin Healey 100 sports car. The other was a very tidy unit of 1,200cc that was not unlike the B series, but had a gear-type oil pump and by-pass oil filter, using the crankshaft, connecting rods, pistons, camshaft, and bore centres from the pre-war Austin 10/4 of 1932, of 65.5mm bore and 89mm stroke. It produced 40bhp at 4,300rpm with its Zenith carburettor. This was a good example of tying a designer down to a price. It is *not* an OHV conversion of the Austin 10hp side-valve engine. It was done so the same boring machine could be used to make the new engine. It was fitted to the four-door A40 Devon and two-door Dorset models in 1947, the same year the MG Y type saloon was introduced.

In 1953 it was redesigned into the 1,200cc and 1,489cc B series by Eric Bareham and Jimmy Rix, and this engine went into the A40 Somerset in 1954 (same A40, new body). The 1947–53 Austin 1,200cc engine is not a B series, though it looks similar. The new

*Engine Number (earlier models). The plate bearing the engine number is secured to the right-hand side of the cylinder block, above the oil filter. The number is also stamped on the identification plate and must be quoted with the prefix letters and figures*

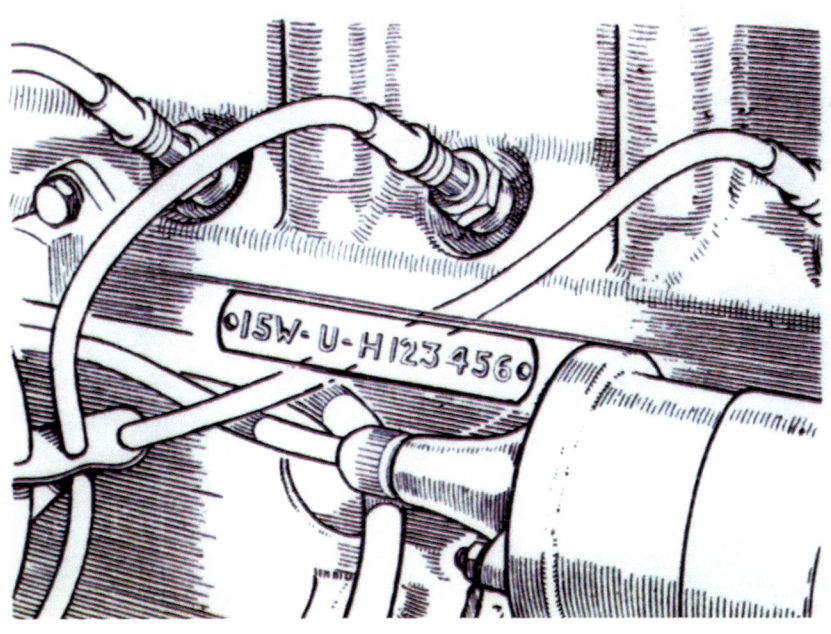

Engine numbering. (BMHIT)

# FITTING VALVE SEAT INSERTS

Should the valve seatings become so badly worn or pitted that the normal workshop cutting and refacing tools cannot restore them to their original standard of efficiency, special valve seat inserts can be fitted.

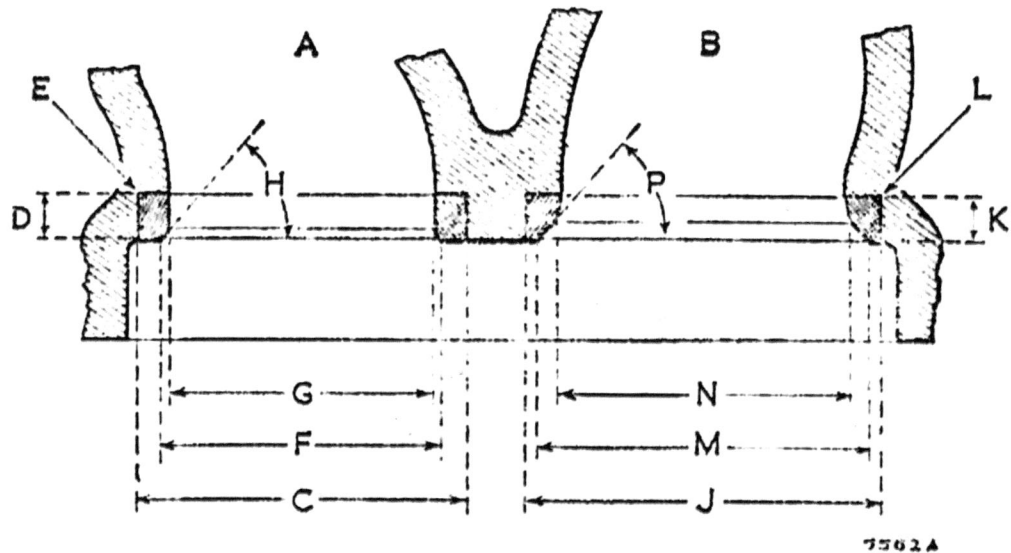

*Fig. A.11*

*Valve seat machining dimensions*

Exhaust (A)
- C. 1·312 to 1·313 in. (33·32 to 33·35 mm.).
- D. ·186 to ·188 in. (4·72 to 4·77 mm.).
- E. Maximum radius ·015 in. (·38 mm.).
- F. 1·221 to 1·241 in. (31·01 to 32·12 mm.).
- G. 1·0805 to 1·1005 in. (27·44 to 27·95 mm.).
- H. 45°.

Inlet (B)
- J. 1·437 to 1·438 in. (36·50 to 36·52 mm.).
- K. ·186 to ·188 in. (4·72 to 4·77 mm.).
- L. Maximum radius ·015 in. (·38 mm.).
- M. 1·396 to 1·316 in. (35·46 to 35·97 mm.).
- N. 1·240 to 1·260 in. (31·50 to 32·00 mm.).
- P. 45°.

The hardened steel valve-seat inserts required today to cope with unleaded fuel. (BMHIT)

# THE ENGINE

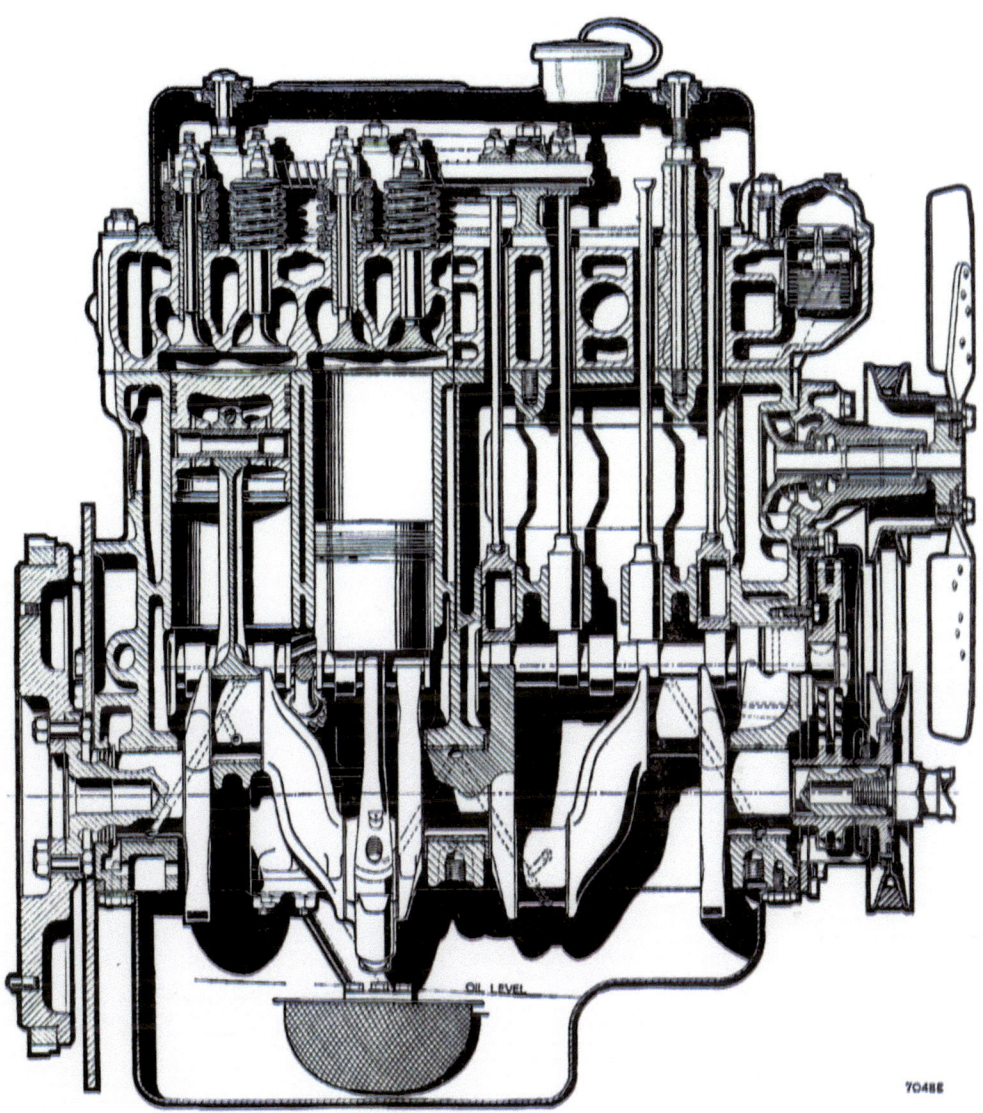

The BMC B series, made in their millions worldwide. (BMHIT)

redesigned engine was of conservative design, in grey cast iron, with a pressed steel sump, timing chain cover and rocker cover. Its mechanical petrol pump was driven off a lobe on the camshaft and it was a push-rod OHV unit with heart-shaped bath-type combustion chambers that were developed by the same consultant who had a hand in the A series – Harry Weslake. The cylinders were further apart than the original A40 1,200cc engine and the crankshaft was of EN16 carbon steel. The 89mm stroke meant

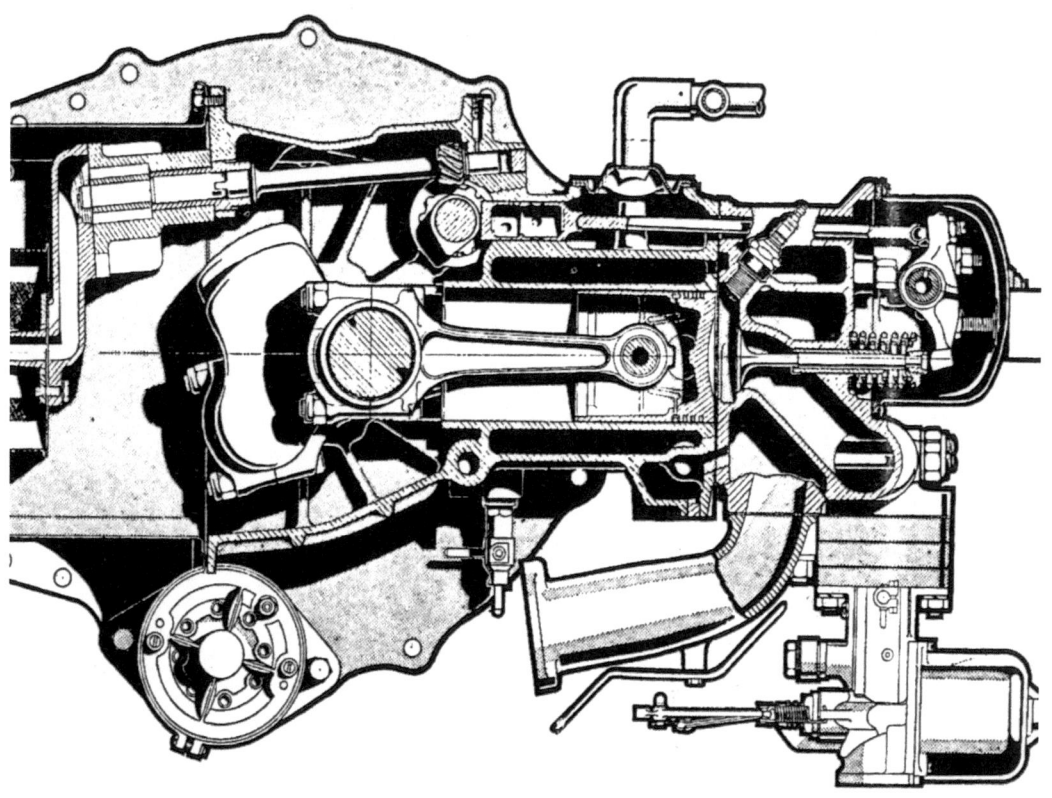

The BMC B series. (BMHIT)

the counterweights of the crank actually went within 1/16 of an inch of the camshaft – something that limited any lengthening of the stroke in later life. It was only designed for a five-year production life after all. All A and B series engines had their compression ratios altered, within that engine's model range, by the differing dish in the piston. This made production easier as only one cylinder head was required, and should you have an engine with a flat piston this would be a high-compression version. The cylinder head had five ports and all four inlets were siamesed into two, and the two centre exhausts shared a port, just as in the MPJG Midget engine of 1936. This central exhaust port would mean the exhaust valves would run very hot, so only the best steel was used in them. Even so, many larger B series developed a name for running on after switching the ignition off, easily cured today by fitting an anti-run-on valve from a Metro to the inlet manifold (this lets air in directly on switching off the ignition). The camshaft design ensured the cams lasted a lot longer than the XPAG versions. The camshaft was slightly offset from the centreline of the followers above, so as the cam lobe rotated and lifted the follower; being offset, it rotated the follower as well inside its bore. This reduced wear of both parts considerably as multiple areas took the stress, and it stopped the pocketing of the follower's lower face.

Like the A series, it had all the electrics on one side of the block and fuel on the other for safety. The original B series had a paper/felt element oil filter in a bolt-on steel bowl, but it was still only a by-pass version, taking 10 miles to filter all the oil just once. A by-pass filter has a small feed from the main oil gallery exiting into the sump, the main feed not going though it. A full-flow one filters all the oil going to the bearings. Early by-pass engines have no oil pipe to this filter, which assists identification. The pipe was fitted to modify the by-pass filter to a full-flow one. The oil pump was an eccentric three-lobe type by Hobourn-Eaton, driven from a skew gear off the camshaft, with the distributor drive coming off the same gear via a jack-shaft that sits between the cylinders. This means the distributor is at an angle on the other side of the engine. Oil pressure was controlled by a valve by the oil filter at the rear. It is easy to add a few washers to the spring to boost a low pressure when selling the car, beware. Connecting rods (con-rods) had the pinch-bolt gudgeon pin and diagonally split big-ends so they could be withdrawn up through the cylinder. On old long-stroke SV engines it was common to drop the sump, undo the big ends and wriggle the piston down past the crankshaft; OHV engines usually have pistons that are too big for this, having much broader bores. The 89mm stroke was to give the engine good mid-range torque, but would limit rpm and development; not that the designer had any idea his engine would still be being built in the 1980s. It had three main bearings on its counterbalanced crankshaft that were a larger diameter than the A40 1200 unit of 1947. The timing chain had a tensioner, which the earlier engines before 1954 did not. The 1,200cc version only lasted until 1957, but the 1,489cc was still in use in the Wolseley 1500 as late as 1965. Of all engines, the B is the easiest to identify, as they have their capacity cast in numbers on the nearside front of the block under the dynamo: '1200' for 1,200cc and '1500' for 1,489cc for these early units, then '1600' for 1,588cc, '1622' for 1,622cc and '1800' for 1,798cc. It is one of the heaviest engines about for its size: 370lbs for a 1,489cc, less gearbox; 520lbs for a 1,798cc with gearbox.

As Austin and Morris had amalgamated, both had huge engineering capacity, and the A and B were built by Morris Engines at Longbridge, now the BMC Engines Division. Austin also used good quality metals in their cars and mechanics, and both firms had excellent reputations for good service and long life of their engines. Austins, for instance, could go for 100,000 miles, whilst current Ford side-valves of the time were often worn out at 35,000. The B series was a hardworking, long-lasting unit, a name that became a byword for reliability, if not high power. The B does leak oil, especially early units that have the felt front timing cover seal and the rear reverse-scroll seal. Slight crankcase compression and a bit of wear will allow this rear seal to weep and leave you a little signature on the clean drive via the bell housing drain hole. Later engines had a modern front seal, but it was not until the 1800 five main bearing MGB/Marina engine did we get a decent neoprene sprung rear seal. MG were once again to take a bread-and-butter engine and use it to advantage in their sports car and saloons.

There is a lot of the B series in early Nissan-Datsun cars, as they assembled CKD export Austin 1,200cc A40 Devons and 1,489cc A50 Cambridges in the early 1950s. Later Nissan built the A55 complete as well as the B series engine. They later updated this engine to their own cars. Morris did this in the 1930s to the Ford SV engine in the Model Y, copying it for his Morris Eight but as a mirror image.

# Known Engine Modifications During Production

Because of the sheer number of vehicles the B series engine was fitted to over a long period, only an overview is given. Use your own car's manual for accurate information.

| Date | Model | Modification |
|---|---|---|
| October 1953 | MG ZA Magnette | New 1,489cc B series engine |
| January 1954 | All | Reynolds timing chain tensioner fitted |
| October 1954 | Austin A40 and A50 | Gain 1,200 and 1,489cc engines |
| October 1954 | Oxford S2 and Cowley S2 | Gain 1,200 and 1,489cc engines |
| 1955 | All | Oil pump output increased |
| 1956 | All | Full flow oil filter fitted |
| 1956 | Austin and Morris | 1,200 discontinued, but carried on in Eire in the A50 until 1959 |
| 1958 | All | Vent pipe from crankcase given a swan neck to stop oil loss |
| 1958 | MG MGA | 1,489 bored out to 1,588cc for use in MGA Twin Cam and MGA 1600 |
| November 1958 | All | Exhaust manifold improved, and Austins lose their Zenith carbs for SU, increasing power by 2bhp |
| 1959 | BMC | Australia develop the 1,622cc engine |
| 1960 | Austin and Morris | 1,489cc diesel version |
| September 1961 | Farina models and MGA | 1,622cc introduced in UK, bigger valves, stronger engine |
| June 1962 | MGB 1800 | 1,798cc three main bearing, 18G and 18GA fitted to new MGB |
| February 1964 | MGB-export | Closed circuit breather system |
| October 1964 | FWD Austin 1800 | 1,798cc engine used in forward transverse location. Five main bearings on crankshaft. |
| October 1964 | MGB | Five main bearing engine, 18GB, rear oil seal on crankshaft, and fully floating gudgeon pins |
| 1965 | Riley 1.5 and Wolseley 1500 | Last 1,489 in saloon car, but it carried on in the vans until 1969 |
| November 1966 | Farina and MGB | Bits of 1,622 and 1,798cc engines commonised, water pump, sump, and larger capacity oil pump. Now 16AA and 16GF. |
| 1968 | 1800 'S' | Biggest inlet valve head fitted, 1.625" dia, 12H2708. Smaller combustion chamber, most powerful standard B. |
| August 1970 | MGB | North America Emission Control fitted |
| August 1970 | MGB and Austin/Morris 1800 | Closed circuit breather now fed into carb body for UK market |
| 1971 | MGB and Marina 1800 | Engines standardised, now 18V |

| Date | Model | Modification |
|---|---|---|
| April 1971 | Farina and MGB | Last 1,622cc engine |
| 1975 | MGB | Gains a catalytic converter for USA market |
| 1978 | Marina 1800 | Last Morris car with a B |
| 1978 | Princess s2 | First use of O series |
| October 1980 | MGB | Last MGB |
| 1980 | Sherpa | Last B series |

## B Series Camshafts in MG Engines

| Model | Cam Timing | Lift | Part No. | Inlet | Exhaust Valves |
|---|---|---|---|---|---|
| ZA Magnette to 18101 | 5;45;40;10 | .312" | 48G184 | 1.375" | 1.28" |
| ZA and ZB Magnette | 5;45;40;10 | .312" | 48G184 | 1.5" | 1.28" |
| All MGA | 16;56;51;21 | .355" | 88G252 | 1.5" | 1.28" |
| MGA Twin Cam | 20;50;50;20 | ? |  | 1.6" | 1.44" |
| Mk3 Magnette to 8067 | 5;45;40;10 | .312" | 48G184 | 1.5" | 1.28" |
| Mk3 and Mk4 Magnette | tdc;50;35;15 | .312" | 12H76 | 1.5" | 1.28" |
| MGB, MGB GT | 16;56;51;21 | .355" | 88G303 | 1.56" | 1.34" |
| MGB after Oct '67 | 16;56;51;21 | .355" | 12H2746 | 1.625" | 1.34" |

The lift on the chart is at the valve, as the rockers act at a ratio of 1.4, the actual lift on the cam lobe is .220" for a .312" lift, and .250" for a .355" lift. The part numbers of BMC change at lot for the same item, depending upon the supplier, hence a 12H76 is also a 12H34. A 48G184 is also a 1H603, 1G2591, 1H1066, and a 88G252 can be a 88G303, 12H2746, 1H1435, 1H729, 12H1647, and 12H1656. Clear as mud now?

The big inlet valve head of the post-1967 MGB is the one standardised with the Austin 1800 S. Cylinder heads are like those of the A series. Any B head will fit any B series engine from 1,200cc in 1953 to 1,798cc in 1980. This sounds good until you note the valve and combustion chamber sizes, some swaps produce vintage compression ratios, other cause the inlet valve to hit the block with serious results. An easy check point of a 1,798cc cylinder block with the head off is the small scalloped out radii in the side of the bore, there to give clearance to that inlet valve's edge. This scallop is required if fitting an 1800 head to any other engine. An 1800 cylinder head has the number 18 cast at the rear end, behind the rocker cover, to assist you in identifying it, and like the 1,275cc head, it is slightly longer than the smaller engines. Late Marina 1.8 heads, if used, use a different rocker post for the oil supply to the rockers – look for the oil feed hole in the head.

## B Cylinder Heads

They are easy to swap about, so what is fitted to your car? Only a general picture is given here, using the combustion chamber capacity.

| Engine Size | Chamber CC | Comp Ratio | Part No. (if known) |
|---|---|---|---|
| 1,200cc saloons | 38cc | 8.3 or 7.2 | ? |
| 1,489cc saloons | 39cc | 8.3 or 7.2 | 48G241 |
| 1,489cc commercials | 39cc | 7.2 | 48G241 |
| 1,489cc MG/Riley | 39cc | 9.0, 8.3 or 7.2 | 12H1670 |
| 1,622cc saloons | 43cc | 8.3 or 7.2 | 12H1670 |
| 1,622cc MG/Riley | 43cc | 8.9 or 8.3 | 12H1670 |
| 1,622cc commercials | 43cc | 8.3 or 7.2 | 12H1670 |
| 1,798cc MGB | 43cc | 9.0 or 8.1 | 12H1326 |
| 1,798cc MG/Marina | 43.5cc | 9.0 or 8.1 | 12H2706, 12H2709 |
| 1,798cc commercials | 43.5cc | 9.0 or 6.9 | 12H2709 |
| 1,798cc 18V and 18H | 43.5cc | 9.0 or 8.0 | 12H4735 offset oil feed |
| 1,798cc 1800 S | 37cc | 9.5* | 12H2708 |

* Bigger 1.625-inch-diameter inlet valve. The last shown, on the Austin 1800s, with its smaller 37cc combustion chamber, is very hard to source. The part number is cast into the head, under the rocker cover, between the valve springs. Remember, the compression ratio is controlled by the piston crown in B series engines. As early engines had tiny valves, I cannot imagine anyone wanting to fit one to an MGB. The five main bearing heads have better combustion chamber shapes – very wide and little valve masking.

Part numbers may well be cast into the heads.

# B Series Through the Years

This shows how the power rose and bores got larger as years went by, and their centres were put further and further apart, siamesing the cylinder block bores and offsetting the big end journals to the bores.

| Model | Year | BHP | Max Speed (mph) | Bore/Stroke (mm) |
|---|---|---|---|---|
| Austin A40 | 1954 | 42 | 65 | 65.5/89 |
| MG Magnette ZA | 1954 | 60 | 81 | 73 |
| MGA 1500 | 1955 | 72 | 99 | 73 |
| Austin A55 Cambridge | 1957 | 51 | 80 | 73 |
| Wolseley 1500 | 1957 | 50 | 80 | 73 |
| Morris Cowley | 1957 | 42 | 65 | 65.5 |
| Morris Oxford | 1957 | 55 | 74 | 73 |
| MG Magnette ZB | 1958 | 68 | 87 | 73 |
| Austin A55 Mk2 | 1959 | 53 | 79 | 73 |
| Riley 4/68-Mk3 Mag | 1959 | 68 | 85 | 73 |
| MGA 1600 | 1959 | 80 | 101 | 75.4 |
| MGA Twin Cam | 1960 | 108 | 113 | 75.4 |

| Model | Year | BHP | Max Speed (mph) | Bore/Stroke (mm) |
|---|---|---|---|---|
| MGA 1600 Mk2 | 1961 | 93 | 103 | 76.2 |
| MG Magnette Mk4 | 1962 | 72 | 88 | 76.2 |
| Austin A60 | 1962 | 61 | 81 | 76.2 |
| MGB | 1964 | 95 | 106 | 80.26 |
| Morris Marina 1.8 | 1972 | 85 | 95 | 80.26 |
| Morris Marina 1800 TC | 1973 | 95 | 101 | 80.26 |
| Austin 1800 S | 1974 | 96 | 102 | 80.26 |

Note: The year quoted is that of the road test giving the maximum speed.

With BMC building the B series, Nissan in Japan building them as well as those built in Argentina over 5 million were produced.

## MG Magnette Mk3 Engine 1958 to 61 (Riley 4/68)

The B series was in use in lots of cars, one being perhaps a controversial MG model. No matter what your views, the car is part of MG history and was part of a range of MGs for the public. This model has the 1,489cc 15GE engine, a very close relative to the MGA 1500 engine of 68bhp, the engine being shared with a sister car, the Riley 4/68, and a tiny Riley 1.5 model based on a Morris Minor floor pan (with huge drum brakes). The Mk3 has two SU HD4 1½-inch carburettors on an engine that is identical to the ZB Magnette, the carbs being the only difference and have a rubber diaphragm for mixture and choke control, not fitted to any other MG (but fitted in a HD6 size to Jaguar, Rover and Rolls-Royce cars). It has an 8.3 to 1 compression and the 68bhp is at 4,800 rpm and 85lb/ft torque at 3,300rpm, the camshaft being a bit softer for saloon use and of 5;45;40;10 valve timings, with a lift of .322". The normal Austin A60 versions have the standard BMC cam of 5;45;45;5 with .0312" lift, and 60bhp. The inlet valve is 1.5" diameter and the exhaust 1.28". The engine has to work very hard indeed to pull the 23cwt saloon. At engine number 15GE 8067 the camshaft timing was altered to TDC;50;35;15, which was moving it all along five degrees to improve torque, something they did with the standard MG Midget cam timing on the MG Metro 1300 later. Oil pressure was 75psi, not the normal 50psi of the single carb models. The Mk3 did not use the tachometer drive off the cam, so it was left un-drilled. The Riley cars did use it. 2,889 Di Tella Farina Magnette 1622s were built in Argentina between 1960 and 1967. These were either single or twin carburetted, with plastic dashboards.

## MG Magnette Mk4 Engine 1961–68 (Riley 4/72)

In October 1962 the Mk4 Magnette gained the MGA 1600 Mk2 engine but detuned to 72bhp in the interests of longer life and mid-range torque. Camshaft, valve sizes and carburettors remained as the Mk3. With bore and stroke of 76.2mm and 89mm, and an 8.3:1 compression, the engine produced 72bhp at 5200rpm with 89lb/ft torque. The fan had four blades fitted from November 1964 – two previously. In November

1966 the 1,622cc engines had common parts from the MGB/Marina 1800 fitted to cut down costs and stocks. The sump was enlarged to one side to accommodate the bulge in the block that now housed the bigger MGB oil pump and was in fact an MGB sump, and the MGB water pump was fitted. The engine was prefixed 16GF. The Riley 4/72 lost its camshaft/cable-driven MGA/early MGB tacho on its 16RA engine, and had an electronic impulse unit fitted. It too then had the common 16GF engine, now fitted to both Farinas. Both cars benefit from an 88°C thermostat, as they tend to run cool on the standard 82°C one. The 1,622cc engine gave the large saloon a decent performance and it could touch 90mph if you were brave! If you wish to fit a MGB 1798cc engine to a Farina Magnette (or to an MGA come to that) try to locate a 18G or 18GA MGB three main bearing engine. These will bolt directly onto the Farina/MGA's gearbox. The later five main bearing unit requires the smaller car's rear engine plate turning out on a lathe to take the rear neoprene (and much improved) crankshaft oil seal and the old oil drain on the plate brazing up, the smaller car's gearbox first motion shaft shortening by ¾ inch as well as a smaller 1,622/1,498cc engines sintered bronze bush fitting into the spigot bearing hole in the rear of the crank. The flywheels of the smaller engines have different fixing bolt spacings to the later five main bearing 1,798cc, so the MGB flywheel has to be used, with it drilled accurately to take the 8-inch Farina clutch cover. Use a Farina clutch plate, so it will match the gearbox splined first motion shaft. Yes, quite a bit of modification.

When the other single-carburettor Farinas gained the MGB engine parts, they were called 16AA engines. The Mk3 and Mk4 Magnette produced 30,996 cars, and very few survive. Some were automatic cars, using the Borg Warner type 35 automatic gearbox – the same unit as in the MGB automatic. Only 300 Mk4s were made in their last year of production.

## Almost Fitted to Farina MGs

### 1,622cc Compliments of BMC Australia and the Blue Streak

The year 1959, the same year that BMC introduced the Mini, saw the engine design department produce an updated B of 1,622cc. It was actually built by BMC Australia, as they thought the 1,489cc too small for their needs. The engine was thoroughly tested down under, but they went one stage further by adding two more cylinders to the block and calling it the 2,433cc Blue Streak Six, keeping the same 1,622cc bore centres, cylinder bore and stroke. This unit was what they needed to fit the Farina A60 Austin and Wolseleys they assembled there. The competition was the Holden, Ford Falcon and GM Valiant. Moving the engine back a bit and the front suspension cross member forward 1 inch to improve weight distribution, the six-cylinder sold against the big American economy sixes and V8s as the Austin Freeway and Wolseley 12/80. BMC in the UK did not want to know, having tried the same idea with a six from 1,489cc earlier. So it became a small six peculiar to Australia, producing 80bhp at 4,800rpm on a single SU HS2 carburettor. A B that never officially got into an MG. This six cylinder is not a C series; that was designed by the Morris part of BMC. A Blue Streak Six was borrowed and used in the MGC in the prototype for measurements and road testing the new torsion bar ifs. MG called this 2,433cc the 'light-six' B series.

A six-cylinder development of BMC Australia was the core engine for the later C series, seen here in an MGC (those pancake air filters are a bit thin and might restrict the carburettors).

## Use of the B Series

The BMC B series engine was used in a massive number of vehicles. Here is a list to assist in identifying them. Note that engine numbers on second-hand units are often chiselled off – possibly to hide its origin. Early A40 used a 1,200cc engine that is not a B series.

| Model | CC | Prefix | BHP/RPM | Torque |
|---|---|---|---|---|
| Austin A40 Devon | 1,200 | BP12A | 40/4300 | 58 lb/ft |
| Austin A40 Somerset | 1,200 | BP12A | 42/4500 | 58 |
| Austin A40 Sports | 1,200 | BP12A | 42/4500 | 58 |
| Austin A40 Sports | 1,200 | BP12A | 46/4500 | 58 |
| Morris Cowley Series 1 | 1,200 | BP12M | 40/4500 | 58 |
| Austin/Nash Metropolitan 1200 | 1,200 | BP12A | 40/4500 | 58 |
| Austin/Nash Metropolitan 1500 | 1,489 | BP15A | 52/4500 | 70 |
| Nash Metropolitan USA version | 1,489 | 15F | 52/4500 | 72 |
| Morris Oxford Series 2 | 1,489 | BP15MH | 50/4500 | 70 |
| Morris Oxford Series 2 (low comp) | 1,489 | BP15ML | 45/4500 | 65 |

| Model | CC | Prefix | BHP/RPM | Torque |
|---|---|---|---|---|
| Morris Cowley Series 2 | 1,489 | BP15M | 50/4500 | 70 |
| Morris Oxford Series 3 | 1,489 | 15M | 55/4500 | 72 |
| Morris Oxford Series 4 | 1,489 | 15M | 55/4500 | 72 |
| Wolseley 15/50 | 1,489 | BP15W | 50/4500 | 70 |
| Wolseley 15/50 | 1,489 | 15AMW | 55/4500 | 72 |
| Wolseley 1500 Mk1 | 1,489 | BP15LAW | 50/4500 | 70 |
| Wolseley 1500 Mk2 | 1,489 | 15W, 15WA | 55/4500 | 72 |
| Riley 1.5 Mk1 | 1,489 | 15R, 15RA | 60/4800 | 77 |
| Riley 1.5 Mk2 | 1,489 | 15RB | 66/5200 | 82 |
| MG Magnette ZA * | 1,489 | BP15GA | 60/4600 | 77 |
| MG Magnette ZB | 1,489 | BP15GC | 68/5200 | 82 |
| MG MGA | 1,489 | BP15GB | 68/5200 | 82 |
| MG MGA | 1,489 | BP15GD | 72/6000 | 85 |
| MG MGA Twin Cam | 1,588 | BC16GB | 108/6700 | 104 |
| MG MGA 1600 | 1,588 | 16GA | 80/5600 | 87 |
| J Type ½-ton Commercial Van | 1,489 | BP15ML, 15AC | 50/4200 | 74 |
| Diesel Engine | 1,489 | BP15J, 15Y, 15Z | 40/4200 | 90 |
| Austin A50 Cambridge | 1,489 | 1H | 50/4500 | 70 |
| Austin A55 Cambridge | 1,489 | 15 | 55/4500 | 72 |
| Austin A55 Cambridge Mk2 (Farina) | 1,489 | 15AMW | 55/4500 | 82 |
| Morris Oxford Series 5 (Farina) | 1,489 | 15AMW | 55/4500 | 82 |
| Wolseley 15/60 (Farina) | 1,489 | 15AMW | 55/4500 | 82 |
| Riley 4/68 (Farina) | 1,489 | 15RA, 15RB | 68/5200 | 85 |
| MG Magnette Mk3 (Farina) | 1,489 | 15GE | 66/5200 | 85 |
| Morris Oxford Series 6 (Farina) | 1,622 | 16AMW, 16AA | 61/4500 | 90 |
| Di Tella (Argentina) (Farina) | 1,489 | 15AMW | 55/4500 | 82 |
| Austin Cambridge A60 (Farina) | 1,622 | 16AMW, 16AA | 61/4500 | 90 |
| Wolseley 16/60 (Farina) | 1,622 | 16AMW, 16AA | 61/4500 | 90 |
| MG Magnette Mk4 (Farina) | 1,622 | 16GE, 16GF | 68/5200 | 89 |
| Riley 4/72 (Farina) | 1,622 | 16RA, 16GF | 72/5500 | 90 |
| MG MGA 1600 Mk2 | 1,622 | 16GC | 92/5500 | 97 |
| A60 ½-ton Commercials | 1,622 | 16AC, 16AE | 61/4500 | 90 |
| Farinas with Alternators, '71 only | 1,622 | 16C | 61/4500 | 90 |
| BMC ½-ton Van | 1,622 | 16AD | 61/4500 | 90 |
| BMC 'B' Gold Seal Recon-engines | All | 48G | | |
| Sherpa Van, Low Compression | 1,622 | 16V | 58/4500 | 82 |
| Sherpa Van, Low Compression | 1,798 | 18V | 80/5000 | 85 |
| Morris Marina 1800 | 1,798 | 18V | 85/5000 | 90 |
| Morris Marina 1800 TC | 1,798 | 18V | 95/5400 *** | 110 |

| Model | CC | Prefix | BHP/RPM | Torque |
|---|---|---|---|---|
| Austin 1800 Mk1 | 1,798 | 18C, 18AMW | 80/5000 | 90 |
| Morris 1800 Mk1 | 1,798 | 18C, 18AMW | 80/5000 | 90 |
| Wolseley 18/85 | 1,798 | 18C, 18AMW | 80/5000 | 90 |
| All fwd 1800 Mk2 | 1,798 | 18C, 18WB | 86/5300 | 92 |
| All fwd 1800 Mk3 | 1,798 | 18H | 86/5300 | 95 |
| Austin 1800s | 1,798 | 18H | 96/5400 | 106 |
| MG MGB three main bearings | 1,798 | 18G, 18GA | 95/5400 | 110 |
| MG MGB five main bearing | 1,798 | 18GB, 18GD, 18GG, 18GH, 18GF, 18GJ, 18GK, 18GJ, 18GC & 18V | 95/5400 ** | 110 |
| Hindustani 1500 | 1,489 | ? | 50/4200 | 74 |
| Navigator Marine | 1,489 | ? | 42/4200 | 60 |
| Navigator Marine | 1,622 | ? | 58/4500 | 85 |
| Massey Harris Harvester | 1,200 | 1HLC | | |

* Our first model with the B series.
** The MGB had lost power down to the low 70s for the USA market by 1980.
*** This is a MGB engine but using a cheaper flow-cast crankshaft. The vehicles using the same engine can quickly be spotted by this list, and the H and V mean Horizontal and Vertical as on the blue print up on a wall in the drawing office. H was a front-wheel drive; V a rear-wheel drive.

By 1956 BMC had made 250,000 B series engines and by 1960 over 3,000,000 had been made. By the end an estimated 6,000,000 B series had been produced, including those of BMC Australia, Datsun in Japan, Hindustani in India and Di Tella in Argentina.

# 8

# Problems with Farinas

There are two main problem areas. The first is the lack of panels available for the MG and Riley models, and both of them can suffer from terminal corrosion. This is a major problem with chassisless, mono-constructed 1950s and 1960s cars, mass produced from mild steel sheet metal, spot welded together with a multitude of mud traps. Luckily, all the underbody panels are shared by the whole range. It is items like front and rear wings, grille, rear lamp units and even indicator lenses that cause the problems. These are special to type. The rarest item is the chrome front side-lamp trims of the Riley, which wrap around the corners of the front wings. Their Mazak alloy casting disintegrates after twenty to thirty years, leaving a thin outer shell that crumbles when touched. The keen restorer needs to hunt out many auto jumbles and eBay to find what they require.

The wood veneer dash can become a mess if water is allowed to get onto it, such as from leaking windscreens. Leather seats also cost a fortune to reupholster. Interior items are often the most expensive to restore, especially when it is polished wood, leather seats and deep pile carpets. No one is going to make much profit out of rebuilding Farinas back to as-new; they just do not demand the values.

Availability of mechanical parts is much better, as MG Specialists stock MGA 1500 and 1600 Mk2 parts, almost identical to the Farina items, but at a cost. The same goes for the gearbox and rear axle. If you struggle to find a decent camshaft, do not use the Austin A55-A60 item, fit a late MGB one. This gives more power and torque, with a loss of a decent idle rpm as this becomes a bit lumpy. The Riley cable-driven tachometer will find spares again, from the MGA and MG specialists. The later impulse version was fitted to the later 1,275cc MG Midget, 1.8 Morris Marina TC, and the later MGB – only the outer case and dial face differ. The post-1961 Austin A60, etc., cylinder head is the same as all the Farina MG and Riley engines.

Gearbox parts are now hard to find, though some MG specialists stock items for the early three-bearing-engined MGA/MGB unit, which has a similar gearbox to the Farina. The synchromesh on second gear wears out. The plastic ball on the lower end of the gear lever falls off. It will be in the oil drain channel under the lever with its spring clip, with it missing the lever is very sloppy.

The major headache is rust. The front valence, the front outriggers, rear outriggers, forward end of the rear spring to chassis fixing, all the sill areas, the jacking points, the flitch plates under the windscreen and the rear edge of the front wings, all rot out. Door bottoms go as well, but are not structural. The join in the rear roof to boot-lid panel, each side of the rear windscreen, rusts away from underneath.

The construction of the underneath of the car was accidentally designed to catch dirt and salt. Hence it corrodes away quite happily and requires regular checking. Waxoyl or a similar treatment is required to keep it in good condition.

A few owners have fitted twin MGB SU HS4 carburettors when they found out how much the HD4 units costs to rebuild. There are two of them as well.

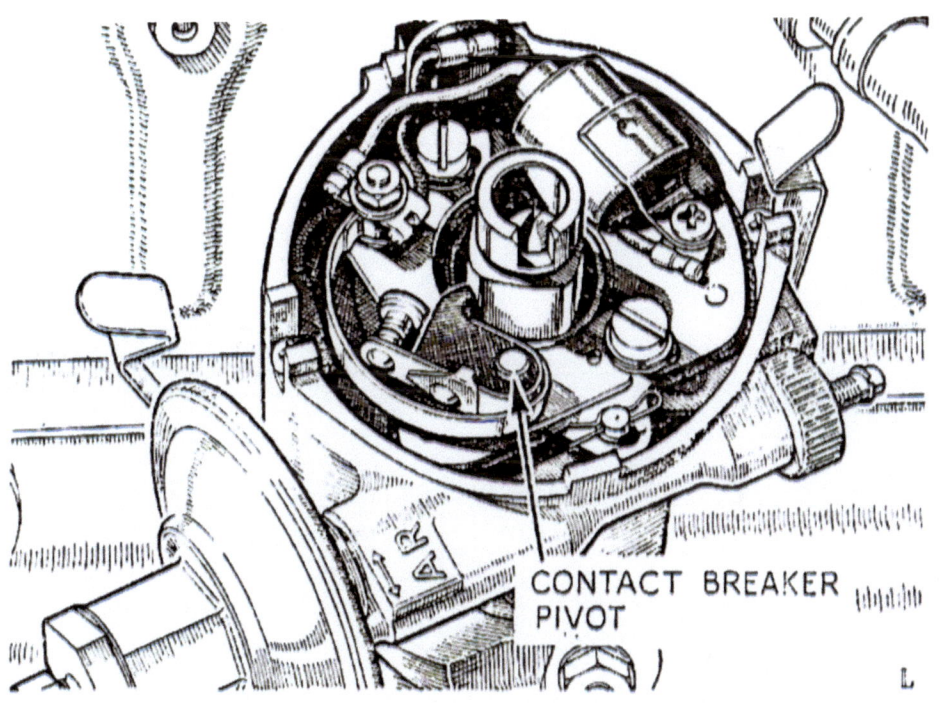

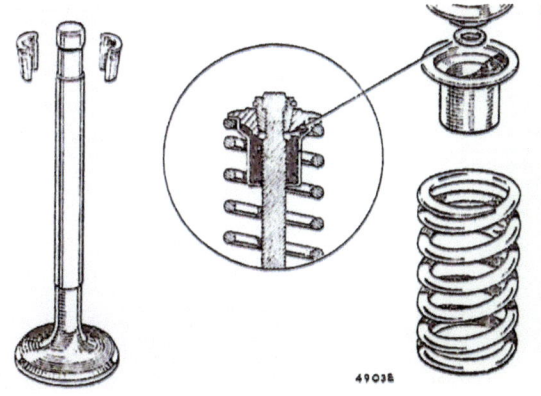

*Above*: Today better reliability can be had by using electronic ignition. Here we have the old points and condenser system. (BMHIT)

*Right*: Valve seals are often incorrectly fitted by amateur (and professional) restorers. If not fitted correctly oil consumption will be excessive. (BMHIT)

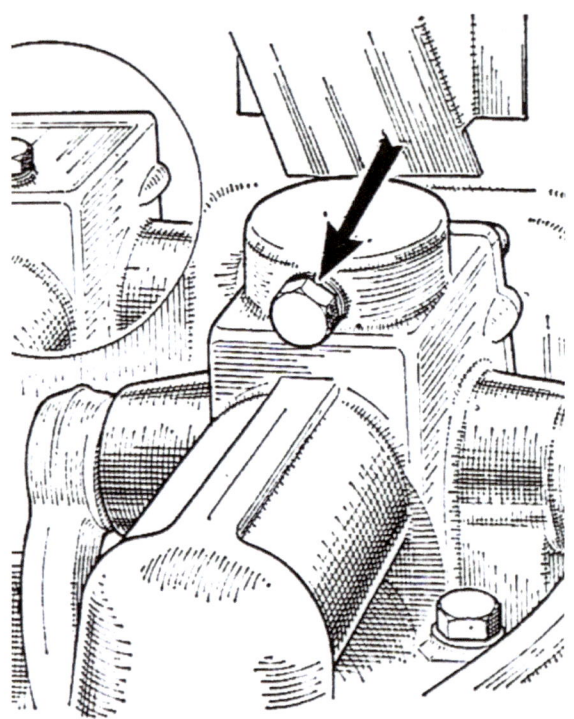

FRONT-DAMPER FILLER PL

*Left*: Lever-arm dampers suffer oil leaks and low oil levels will cause the car to bounce about. They can be exchanged for resealed reconditioned units. (BMHIT)

*Below*: The biggest single problem with these early monocoque cars is rampant corrosion.

Unless the sill repairs have been done correctly, using the jacking points may cause the sill panel to crush and buckle. (BMHIT)

# 9

# The Riley Silhouette and Riviera

In 1961 Wessex Motors Ltd of New Street, Salisbury, a franchised BMC and Riley garage (not Austin), decided to convert the new Farina Riley 4/68 into a more plush, faster and select vehicle. They were to use components from other current BMC cars, so the warranty would not be affected. You purchased your new 4/68 or 4/72 then took it along to them. You were offered three stages of tuning and fittings, depending on the depth of your pocket. The final price was nearly one and a half times the cost of the basic Austin A55 Mk2 saloon, at £1,299 for the full treatment.

## Riley Silhouette

The model carried on with the three stages of tuning and fitting out, but gained the 1,622cc MGA engine. This meant power jumped from 72bhp to 90bhp. It was a good job that the ADO38 now had anti-roll bars, lower suspension, and wider track. Very few 1,622cc MGA-engined cars were made; in fact, it was probably in single numbers as by 1962 the MGB, with its three main bearing 1,798cc engine, had arrived. This big B series used the same gearbox as the MGA and 4/72, so it was an easy fit into the Silhouette. This post-1962 Silhouette was quite a handful, with its 1800 95bhp, 105lb torque engine. Even with the poor drag coefficient of the Farina's body shape, the car would do 100mph easily, whereas the 1,588cc car needed favourable conditions. Acceleration was improved to 0–60 in 12 seconds, cutting the basic Austin/Morris time almost in half.

To differentiate between the two models, the Silhouette had extra chrome side strips running the length of the car, as well as the standard strip on the waist line. This second trim line ran under the other, similar to that on the Austin A60, except it started above the centre of the front wheel arch 18 inches further back, and swept down to follow the rear edge of the rear wheel arch, similar to the Singer Gazelle of the day. The inside area of the side flash could be supplied with a contrasting colour. Nearly all the cars were black, and the flash red. On the most expensive stage three, as well as a tuned 1,798cc engine, the interior seats could be from the Vanden Plas range, with their thick padded, leather covered contours.

By 1964/65 the model was dropped, possibly because the MGB engine gained five main bearings and the new, stronger Sherpa gearbox. The gearbox and clutch of the MGB were now very different to the Farina range's old BMC items. A lot of machining and modifications to the transmission tunnel would be required to fit the bigger four-synchromesh gearbox, bigger flywheel and clutch; or to modify the rear of the engine to fit the older gearbox. The transmission tunnel was not large enough for the new gearbox, or one fitted with overdrive. Soon, the MGB also gained a stronger Salisbury-type rear axle also from the Sherpa van, replacing its BMC banjo axle, the Salisbury one being very different to the Farina BMC item.

One Riviera is known to exist and one Silhouette without its MGB engine. All the cars kept their normal BMC chassis numbering.

Should you want to emulate one of these cars, you can use standard BMC items. You will need an 18G or 18GA MGB engine and manifolding, a Healey 3000 set of stub axles, discs and callipers (similar to the Westminster), a set of MGB wire wheels with splined hub adaptors for all four wheels, early MGB half-shafts for wire wheels (or for a set of bolt-on wire wheels try 0954 231318), spacers for the front and rear suspension (easy to DIY), a Land Rover remote brake-fluid reservoir, an early Allegro/Marina brake servo and the nerve to cut down the rear fins to fit a set of Austin Westminster A99-A110 rear lamp units. *Autocar Magazine* ran a road test of one in the 3 March 1961 issue.

Only one still exists, which was being restored by Mick Holehose. In the book *Cops and Robbers* by Ant Anstead there is a chapter on buying police cars. He mentions both of these specialist Rileys but neither was ever used.

## Riley Riviera

The 4/68 had its engine removed, and an MGA 1600 Mk1 1,588cc unit fitted in its place, either standard or tuned. The large rear fins were cut down to look very like the later A60. Smaller rear lights were fitted. Adjustable Wolseley 15/60 front seats were fitted, of the split-bench type. Spot-lamps were let into the front panel, similar to the big Wolseley 6/99, each side of the grille. The suspension was lowered by three quarters of an inch all round, but anti-roll bars were not fitted. Pirelli Cinturas radial-ply tyres were fitted to the wire wheels of the MGA and these were fitted to Austin Healey 3000 hubs and swivel pins with disc brakes. (The big Healey uses the same suspension as the Farina.) These were then fitted to the Riley 4/68. A remote brake servo was added, fitted to the front nearside of the radiator panel. Because of the large displacement of brake fluid with disc brakes, a larger reservoir was fitted by the battery, with a pipe down to the master cylinder joining where the filler cap had been.

Inside on the dash there was a handbrake warning light, brake fluid level warning light, rear window demister, headlamp flasher and an electric aerial with HMV radio. Extra sound insulation was put under the dash, floor carpets and in the boot. The exhaust was fitted with a Servias silencer. A Riley diamond badge was fitted to the boot-lid, just above the central reversing lamp. The logo, in chrome script RIVIERA, replaced the 4/68 one, on the boot-lid offside.

In a straight line the car could reach 100mph. Gone was the huge oil-bath air filter, MGA pancake ones being substituted, giving better breathing. A tuned MGA cylinder head with polished ports and bigger valves was fitted for the stage-three tuning level. This was plus high compression pistons at 9.5 to 1. The MGA's engine is a straight swap for the Riley unit; both are basically BMC B series 1489cc engines sharing the same gearbox/clutch unit. 0–60mph was given as 14 seconds, compared with a standard 4/68 at 20 seconds. Fuel consumption was in the 22mpg range, compared to the 4/68 at 25–27mpg range.

Alas, nothing was done about the poor handling and steering of the basic 4/68. It is a shame that the rack-and-pinion steering of the MGA was not used as well. Road tests of the time slated the car for it roll-oversteer and poor direction control; tarmac overlaps caused the car to wander trying to follow them.

In 1961 BMC introduced a lot of improvements to the basic ADO9 model, updating it to the ADO38 version. This also improved the cars modified by Wessex Motors automatically. The 1588cc MGA engine was replaced by the MGA 1600 Mk2 engine of 1,622cc and 90bhp, being now fitted into the Riley 4/72. Because this car was so much better, it deserved a change of name. The new Wessex model was to be called the Silhouette.

# 10

# The Di Tella MG

In the 1950s and 1960s Great Britain and Argentina were friends and did a great deal of trade with each other. Should you ever visit Argentina, even today you will still see evidence of the huge amounts of railway furniture we sold to this country. It is almost like looking at our old British Railways back in the 1960s, with copies of our rolling stock and even down to the signalling equipment. Another tie with a part of the UK was the number of Welshmen who emigrated there to become coal miners. Some Patagonian Argentinians still speak a form of Welsh today.

The Di Tella Magnette in Buenos Aires. (Alejandro Mogni)

Dashboard is identical to the UK Farina MG Magnette. (Alejandro Mogni)

At the same time the UK motor industry also gained a hold on that continent and contracts were exchanged for the licensed production of selected BMC models. The Argentinians wanted a solid, dependable and reliable car, that could take the rough roads and rough treatment the locals would meter out. The car would also be sold as an upmarket deluxe saloon. The company who was to build the BMC vehicles was Torcuato Di Tellas Industries of Buenos Aires, whose engineering pedigree dated back to 1910. They had since become a giant industrial company, building things like all that railway rolling stock of British design. Their products also encompassed steel making, electrical motors, cranes, ships, trains and now motorcars.

With BMC technical support Di Tella were to build the 1959 Riley version of the Farina saloon car, called a Di Tella 1500, both as a four-door saloon for use as a taxi and a base family model. The Riley was also sold as the Argenta pick-up, a fate many of the older 1500 taxis were converted to in later life. There was a Morris Oxford Traveller in the range, now called a Di Tella Traveller. The engine was the unburstable single carburettor BMC 1,489cc B series also built under licence.

As well as the bread-and-butter model for the masses, there was to be an up-market version of the Farina and Di Tella chose the Mk3 MG Magnette, selling it with the option of either a single or twin SU carburettor set-up. It was called the Di Tella Magnette unsurprisingly. This car had leather seats, fully carpeted interior and was more luxurious than the basic 1500 (Riley) model. Differences to the UK MG Mk3 Magnette were:

| Di Tella Magnette | MG Magnette Mk3 |
|---|---|
| Left-hand drive | Right-hand drive |
| Steering column gear change | Normal MG floor gear change |
| Moulded plastic dashboard | Rosewood veneered dash |
| Bench front seat with central arm rest | Individual bucket seats (ex-ZB) |
| Single colour body only | Duo-tone paint scheme option |
| Huge over-riders both ends | Small A55 Mk2 over-riders |
| Bumper nudge bars both ends | None |
| Hub cap with Di Tella slanted 'S' motif | YB/TD/ZA/ZB MG hub caps |
| Di Tella motif in the radiator grille octagon | Normal MG octagon on grille |
| Unique engine/body numbering | BMC/MG numbering system |
| Body colour headlamp shrouds | Chromed headlamp shrouds |
| Chrome wheel rim belishers | None |
| Single SU HS2; twin an option | Twin SU HD4 |

The Di Tella motif is not unlike a single S from the Second World War German SS emblem. The very strong bumpers and over-riders were necessary due to the parking habits of local drivers and for pushing loose animals out of the way. The sharp Italianate Pinin Farina styling of the car, with its cut-off fins, attracted the attention of the hot-blooded Argentinians – the very opposite view of UK MG enthusiasts at that time. In the Argentinian car the dashboard looked identical to the UK MG version, the same shape and instruments, but was in fact a large plastic moulding.

Many corporate parts were used to modify the Di Tella Magnette for Argentina. The steering column gear change was standard issue on the previous Austin A55 and an option on the Farina Morris Oxford so fitted easily to the car. As the Farina Magnette uses the A55 floor pan and running equipment, the modification already existed. In the UK this column change, normal BMC gearbox was available with an overdrive, but it is not known if this was on offer in South America.

Production was under way by 1960 and cars were pouring out of the Monte Chingolo factory in Provincia de Buenos Aires. Virtually everything was locally made (similar to the Morris Oxford series 3, then being built in India by Hindustani Industries). A few CKD export cars had been used to check out assembly procedures. (CKD is a Complete Knocked Down car, in bits, in a big box and shipped over.)

1962 saw the Di Tella Magnette update with the MG Mk4 Magnette 1,622cc engine, though the 1500 continued unchanged with its 1,489cc version. It is not yet known if the cars were updated as in the UK, with the longer MK4 wheelbase and suspension improvements (though I suspect not on this locally produced car). The bigger engined Magnette 1622 still had the option of single or twin carburettors, but the rear axle had been changed. The Di Tellas now used an American-sourced rear axle on the cars, a Kaiser version built by a local company called Dana.

Just as in the UK the Magnette versions of the Farina are now rare in Argentina. The Riley based 1500 lasted longer, however, and spares were plentiful for some years. Taxi drivers loved the 1500 car because of its strength and durability and are responsible for

*Above*: Di Tella 1500 that uses the Riley Farina body modified into a pick-up. (Alejandro Mogni)

*Below*: Di Tell Magnette. (Alejandro Mogni)

keeping them on the roads so long. (A little like the Morris 1000 Vans that were still in use in Ceylon in the 1990s, now called Sri Lanka.)

In May 1966 Di Tella sold the motor car production factory to Industrias Kaiser Argentina (IKA), an offshoot of Kaiser Automotores, an American-owned company. Production continued for a few more years but faded out as large American cars took over the market (just as they did in Australia, causing BMC's operations to close there).

Production of the Argentinian MG between 1960 and May 1966 was 2,654 cars. From IKA only 235 MG models were built. Compare these figures to the 45,000 Di Tella 1500s and 2,537 IKA 1500s. The Traveller estate car and Argenta pick-up numbers are not known, but are probably in excess of 30,000.

The few remaining Di Tella Magnette and the later Magnette 1622 are now being collected by MG enthusiasts in Argentina. One enthusiast is MGCC member Alejandro Mogni of Cordoba, Argentina, who already owns a 1946 MG TD, a 1947 MG Y, a 1959 MGA 1500 (under restoration) and now a 1966 Di Tella Magnette 1622 (awaiting restoration,) who supplied the information for this article.

In the UK the poor MG Farina Magnette had a low image, but in South America its sister car was a desirable and upmarket limousine.

An MG club show in Argentina with a Di Tella on display. (Alejandro Mogni)

Di Tella Magnette showing off its rear fins.

# 11

# The Past and the Future

The fact that the Farina Riley and MG exists was because of the policy of BMC to use one basic car to supply five different franchises, just as current manufacturers do today offering different levels of trim and engine size for one body. The water had been tested by BMC in 1953 with the Palmer designed Wolseley 4/44 and MG Magnette Z series. MG sold over 30,000 Z and Wolseley 36,000 4/44s in a seven-year production run. In 1958 BMC launched the Farina range to its garages at a private showing of the Mk3 MG Magnette. In 1959 the Wolseley 15/60 was the first to be shown to the press and public. Today, that very Wolseley 15/60 is the rarest Farina saloon model, with less than sixty on DLVA Swansea's records. The rarest of all the Farinas from BMC are the estate cars, with only four known Austin A55 Mk2 Cambridge Countrymans existing.

In the 1960s the BMC Farina shape was common on our roads that you simply did not notice them. The 900,000 built were part of the British road furniture. In 1971 the last Morris and Wolseley Farinas were built and sold. Some years before the twin carburettor cars had quietly been dropped: the MG in 1968 and the Riley in 1969. No one mourned their loss; no one noticed either. Some of the last cars took some time for the garages to sell off. The cars were just too old fashioned. Underneath your new 1969 Riley 4/72 was the basic floor pan of an Austin Cambridge designed in 1952.

By the 1980s the Farina cars were old bangers and many had gone to scrap yards. Not many were now seen as every day cars. Both the MG and Riley were being brought for their basically MGA engine and gearbox for just a few pounds. Banger racing was rife and Farinas were a popular choice as they were very strong. Such cars were wrecks anyway – no one was restoring a Farina in those days.

The 1990s were the lean years. So few MG and Riley cars were on the roads that even national rallies of the various clubs that supported them would only see two or three attend. Younger generations of motoring enthusiasts were surprised to see large 1960s MG family saloons at an MG rally. Many did not even know such a car existed.

Compared with the numbers of Austin, Morris and Wolseley Farinas, fewer of the twin carburettor MG and Riley cars were sold. In the last year of production in 1968 of the Mk4 Magnette saw just 300 off the lines. No manufacturer is going to bother with such low numbers; they simply became uneconomic. Today the Riley 4/68 is the second rarest Farina saloon, followed in order by the Mk3 Magnette, Mk4 Magnette, then the 4/72.

But people are restoring MG and Riley Farinas. Once people do this, there is some hope. NTG of Ipswich supply parts for the cars. Again, the fact someone takes the trouble to do this is good news. Pristine cars are seen at MG and Riley meetings and shows and now people walk over to them to take an interest. Of the very few cars now left, the best ones have become the Cinderella of their class.

Today in the twenty-first century a big Farina MG is a car that will attract attention where ever you go. It is an excellent family car and can carry a huge amount of luggage and four people in comfort. With roads now having 50mph speed limits commonplace and 60 elsewhere, the car has no problem keeping up with modern traffic. On a motorway 70mph cruising is a bit too fast and fuel consumption will be high as the model never saw a wind tunnel during its styling.

You will need your own grease gun. The car has many points that require regular attention, though the later Mk4s less so with some sealed for life items like the universal joints on the propeller shaft. Pump LM grease into the king pins and steering joints until clean grease oozes out. Oil filters and engine oil changes are required at much lower mileage, at 3,000 miles rather than the 12,000 of a modern car. The leather seats will need feeding with leather food or they will dry out and crack.

When it comes to mechanical spares engine, gearbox and rear axle spares are easy to source as the MGA and early MGB used similar items so MG specialists can help. You will need to explain what a Mk3 or Mk4 is though. Suspension parts are similar to the Austin Healey sports cars, so their specialists may have the bit you need. As mentioned NTG of Ipswich carry a huge stock of parts and their catalogue is a must have for any keen owner.

With modern fuel full of ethanol, it is vital the car has its fuel system adapted to cope. Plastic pipes need to be ethanol-proof and the carburettor floats need to be of the Burlen stay-up type. If your car still has the brass floats, the tin in the solder that fixes the two halves together will be dissolved. The ethanol-proof floats can be obtained from Burlen Fuel Services, as can a solid state SU fuel pump. There are no points in these electronic versions to burn out.

By now all cars should have been rewired with modern cables, as the originals will have hardened and cracked and become a fire risk. Most insurance companies offering agreed value cover will ask when the car was rewired. Also, with DVLA giving all old cars Vehicle of Historic Interest (VHI) status, modifying the car beyond their guidelines will remove it from VHI status and the car will have to have an annual MoT. See the DVLA website for more information.

John Elwood runs a website for all known Farinas: www.mgcars.org.uk/farina.

## 90BHP 1,622cc Engine?

If you feel your Mk4 Magnette is not fast enough, you can modify it by getting more engine power as the same basic unit was used in the MGA and MGB. You can carry out engine swaps between cars using the B series. Up to the three-main-bearing 1,798cc MGB engine this is easy. With the 1,798cc MGB five-main-bearing engine things get difficult because they used the stronger Sherpa gearbox requiring a different rear-plate and flywheel. So why not just improve the 1622cc engine already fitted? Typically the Austin A60, Series 6 Morris Oxford and the Wolseley 16/60 all produce a tiny 61 bhp, but the Mk4 MG and 4/72 manage 72 bhp, all with a torque of about 89–90lb/ft. These modifications can also be done to the 1489cc engine using the parts suggested, but it becomes a bit more cammy and harsh.

The MGA 1600 Mk2, made from 1961 to 1962 (and only 8,719 were made), used the same 1,622cc engine as the A60, but in this MG form produced 93bhp and 95lb/ft torque. If you fit the relevant bits that this MGA used, to your A60, Mk4, etc., you too can have quite a powerful motor and you do not even need to take the engine out! What you do is build your present 1,622cc engine up to the MGA specification.

Right from the start let's get something very clear. You will not have a smooth saloon car engine any more. Your insurance will go up. Your engine's condition must be good and you are going to have to do a lot a spanner work. Your A60 engine has some very important limitations, the same the MGA 1600 Mk2 had, and the reasons why the 1800 engine was developed to cure. The cam followers are of the barrel type and the con-rod has a pinch bolt on the little-end (gudgeon pin). This bolt makes the con rod rather weak and limits the power/revs. These arrangements were also in the three main bearing MGB engine (18G and 18GA).

The MG Magnette Z series engine that the Mk3 and 4/68 used.

A Mk4 Magnette engine tuned up to 90bhp.

The engine produces its maximum power at about 4,500 rpm in saloon car tune. The MGA 1600 Mk2 did so at 5,500 rpm. Your engine was designed to last donkeys years, but sports cars get quite regular engine rebuilds. The MGA had disc front brakes; your saloon car has drums. I hope I make my point.

## What Do You Need to Do?

Obtain an 1800 cylinder head from an MGB or Marina. Recondition it if it needs it (a good time to go lead-free by fitting hardened steel valve seat inserts). The 1800 head has huge valves and better ports than our A60, Mk4, etc. On the 1800 the inlet valve will hit the 1622 block because the large combustion-chamber is shallow. You will need to grind out a tiny scallop to clear the edge of the valve. The combustion chambers of the 1800 head are shallower (though both A60 and 1800 have volume of 43cc) and you are going to fit a camshaft with more lift.

With your head off, remove your grille, radiator, and sump. The sump can be removed in-situ if you put 1-inch thick blocks of wood under the engine mounts on the cross member, to lift it. Now take off the timing chain cover, the manifolds and side tappet chest covers. Remove the push-rods and the cam followers. Remove the oil pump and the distributor and its jack-shaft (see your workshop manual). Now carefully pull out the camshaft from the front once you have taken off its chain.

Buy an MGB camshaft, it is identical to the MGA one (less the tachometer drive) with the MGA 1600 Mk2 timing and lift. Also buy, or beg, a set of 1800 18V onwards bucket cam followers and the necessary longer push rods. These bucket followers are the same ones fitted to the 1,275cc A series, which are much lighter than the old type, and hence allow higher revs and less loss of power.

With lots of oil on it, fit the camshaft into your block. Ensure the timing is correct. Fit the pulleys and make sure the oil thrower is fitted the right way round. Refit the oil pump, but make sure it's in good condition. Now buy an MGB oil pressure relief valve spring and swap it with your old one. Your oil pressure will now be up around 70–75psi from its previous 50psi. Fit a new oil filter.

Now you can keep your old pistons, with their 8.3 to 1 compression ratio, or buy and fit MGA 1600 Mk2 pistons with their 8.9 to 1 compression ratio. To use your old ones will be far cheaper and you will lose 3–5 bhp only. Refit the sump with a nice new gasket. Refit the timing chain cover with a new gasket and seal. Fit the distributor with MGB springs on the weights for the advance curve (again not essential, but it helps pulling power).

Now, having fitted the head temporarily with no gasket and no nuts, put the push-rods and followers in, and wind the engine over carefully on the handle to see if the valves clear the block (put plasticine on the valve edge to make a mark), taking it off again to check for marks and relieve the block where necessary. You can now fit it properly, with an 1800 head gasket and bolt it down. Remember to put in the new bucket followers and the longer push rods. Torque down the head. You can use your old rockers, but if you used a Marina cylinder head, make sure the oil drilling in the head lines up with that in the rocker pillar. The Marina's oil feed hole is further forward, and you may have to beg, borrow, or buy a Marina pillar with the extra lug on it. When you buy the head, take the current rockers, then there will be no problem. You need to buy an MGA Long Centre Branch (LCB) exhaust manifold. It will need a sleeve to connect it to your old exhaust system as they are both the same diameter. Removing the rear expansion box helps power and noise. An MGB LCB will fit, but not the standard MGB exhaust system. Fit the two engine side tappet covers before you fit the manifolds.

If you are not doing this to the Riley or MG Farina, the inlet manifold needs to be the standard B series alloy-twin carburettor version, fitted with either MGA, or MGB, or Riley 1.5, or MG ZA or ZB, twin SU carburettors, if you can find any. The Riley and MG Farina already use twin carburettors. Those fitted to the Marina 1.8TC are perfectly OK, but whatever you fit, you will need a pair of K&N pancake air filters with stub-stacks. The MGB rich needle is an ideal starting point to fit, a number 6. N9Y plugs are ideal, as is an 88°C thermostat and a 7psi radiator cap.

Now, with the ignition timing set at about 5° BTDC static and a cable throttle control made up as per the Marina 1800, fill the sump with oil, the radiator with water and start it up. Once you have sorted out the odd faults and got the car onto the road, providing you have followed the instructions, your engine should be making about 85 to 90bhp. It will be a bit rough at idle, so the tick over has to be higher at 950rpm.

The bigger 1,789cc MGB engine in this case tuned up even more.

Yes, the car will fly along if you use the revs. But you really need to get the radiator fitted with an efficient four-core matrix, as the A60 three core will not be capable of cooling the engine efficiently at high speed. Or fit an MGB oil cooler. As with the 1800, you need radial ply tyres and disc brakes if you are rich. A nice alloy rocker cover finishes it all off.

Where do you get the bits? Well, a whole MGA 1600 Mk2 engine can be had on 01954 231318, as can an MGA/MGB LCB exhaust manifold, twin carburettor manifolds, new twin carburettors, K&N filters and MGB camshaft. Ring a few other MG specialists, as prices can vary to your advantage. A cylinder head can be had from MG magazine spares adverts (*MG Enthusiast Magazine* or *MG World* at Smiths) or from specialist scrapyards or even eBay.

## Where to Find More Information

**Spares**
NTG are on 01473 741170 or sales@mgbits.com
Moss can supply engine and gearbox bits, but you need to use their MGA 1500 for the Mk3 and 4/68, and the MGA 1600 for the Mk4 and 4/72. Website: www.moss-europe.co.uk.
Austin Healey specialists
Burlen Fuel Services (www.burlen.co.uk)

## Clubs
Cambridge and Oxford Owners Club
Austin Cambridge and Westminster Owners Club
MG Car Club (Magnette Register)
MG Owners Club (Mk3 and Mk4)
The Riley Motor Club (4/68 and 4/72)

## Articles in Magazines
'Riley 4/68', *Popular Classics*, January 1995.
'Buying a Farina', *Practical Classics*, February 1997. For back issues: 01733 238855.
'MG Farina Saloons', *Classic Car Weekly*, 12 February 1997, 01733 237111.
'Endangered Species', *Classic Car Weekly*, 12 April 1995.
'The Mk4 MG Magnette', *MG Enthusiasts Magazine*, Vol. 6, No. 3; Vol. 14, No. 1; Vol. 2, No. 4, 01924 499261.
'MG Farina Magnettes', *Enjoying MG*, December 1990, Vol. 10, No. 12, 01954 231125.
'The Cinderella MG', April 1995.
'Its all in the Badge', May 1996.
'Pocket History of the Farina MG', *Safety Fast*, May 1996, 01235 555552.
'The Di Tella Magnette', January 1999;
'Farina MG Magnette', *MG World*, October/November 1998, 01737 814311.
*Cops and Robbers* by Ant Anstead, William Collins, page 338–340.
List of Farina models: www.mgcars.org.uk/farina.

The Farinas make an excellent family saloon.

## Books

*Plush Farina Fours,* from TSB on 01473 270376, a collection of road tests.
*Riley 4/68 & 4/72, Olyslager Motor Manual No. 35.*
*MG Magnette Mk3 & Mk4, Olyslager Motor Manual No. 34.*
*MG Magnette,* Unique Books, collection of road tests.
*MG Saloon Cars,* Anders Ditlev Clausager, Bay View Books.
*Magnette Mk3 & Mk4 Workshop Manual,* BMC Publication, ADK4027.
*Magnette Mk3 and Mk4 Service Parts Manual,* BMC Publications, ADK953.
*The Austin* by Barney Sharratt, Haynes.